stacey wolf's
psychic
living

stacey wolf's
psychic
living

―

A Complete Guide to

Enhancing Your Life

with Universal Energy

―

Stacey Wolf

J e r e m y   P .   T a r c h e r / P u t n a m

A member of Penguin Putnam Inc. · New York

Most Tarcher/Putnam books are available at special quantity discounts for bulk purchases for sales promotions, premiums, fund-raising, and educational needs. Special books or book excerpts also can be created to fit specific needs. For details, write Putnam Special Markets, 375 Hudson Street, New York, NY 10014.

Jeremy P. Tarcher/Putnam
a member of
Penguin Putnam Inc.
375 Hudson Street
New York, NY 10014
www.penguinputnam.com

Library of Congress Cataloging-in-Publication Data

Wolf, Stacey.
Stacey Wolf's psychic living : a complete guide to enhancing your life with universal energy / Stacey Wolf.
p.   cm.
ISBN 0-87477-932-4 (alk. paper)
1. Parapsychology.   2. Psychic ability.   3. Psychic ability— problems, exercises, etc.   I. Title.
BF1031.W76   1998   98-29909 CIP
133.8—dc21

Printed in the United States of America
1   3   5   7   9   10   8   6   4   2

This book is printed on acid-free paper. ∞

BOOK DESIGN BY CHRIS WELCH

acknowledgments

I am deeply grateful for all the help I have received in creating this book. First, I thank my editor, Wendy Hubbert, for teaching me how to write a book; for being so available to me every day for nine months; and for not letting me get away with anything.

Then there's Sandra Martin, Joel Fotinos, and Irene Prokop, the literary agent, publisher, and editor who understood my vision and believed in me from the beginning. Joel, Sandra, and Irene, thanks for your support.

I thank Theresa Waltermeyer for teaching me to think big, and Kathy Betz for helping me edit and organize material that would eventually become this book. A pat on the back goes out to my two comedy-writing friends Tommy Koenig and Maureen Mato for helping me polish off all the funny stuff!

I don't want to forget my parents, Harvey and Roberta Wolf, and all their unconditional love. They might not have asked for a psychic daughter, but *this* is the payoff. Thanks, Mom and Dad.

There is a warm place in my heart for all of my friends and clients who not only bugged me to write this down, but completed all the exercises and reported back to me; their stories are strewn throughout this manuscript. Here are a special few: Renato Biribin, Jennifer Lord, Julia Gregory, Richard Soriano, Marilyn Harvey, Marie Stomaszic, Miriam Nelson, Toni Singer, and Michelle Amlong.

Last but not least, I thank my dog, Scarlett. Some of you might think it's crazy to thank a dog; but without her constant affection during the endless hours of writing and rewriting, I might have lost it long ago!

In memory of my grandmother Gilda Freeman,
the most loving woman I have known

contents

———

stacey wolf's
psychic
living

introduction

———

As the twenty-first century looms closer and closer, it's clear that we are in the midst of a psychic renaissance. Open your eyes and look around. Spiritual sleepwalkers everywhere are waking up and smelling the psychic coffee! Get this: At IBM, workers consult a favorite psychic in their off-hours. Bastions of conservatism like Motorola, Hewlett-Packard, and Xerox have hired spiritual advisors to inspire their workers and rejuvenate the workplace. Astrology just hit the cover of *Life* magazine. And according to *Time* magazine, 69 percent of us believe in angels.

Remember hearing your parents talk about est and yoga, wacky meditations and dark séances? Think about it. There hasn't been this much spiritual energy floating about since the sixties.

There's a reason people nowadays are experiencing more meaningful coincidences and odd happenings. Our dreams are way too significant to be random. We're watching more television shows on angels, aliens, and ancient mysteries. We're reading more books on intuition, astrology, and prophecy. We're experimenting with the healing power of crystals and reiki. Yoga has replaced aerobics as the exercise of the moment.

It all has to do with the energy floating around in the universe these days. This energy is like an infinite power station in the sky. It makes the planets rotate around the sun; it turns day into night. It is the energy in our bodies, making our hearts beat and our blood flow. In the sixties, our parents were overtaken by the need to spread peace, love, oneness, and freedom. These concepts are manifestations of the energy that links human beings to the universe's higher forces.

During these years—the sixties and seventies—you and I were born into this energy. What this means—hold onto your hat—is that we were *born psychic*. Those of us now in our late twenties and early thirties—Generation X, for want of a better term—came into this world with psychic energy already wired into our brains! We have an innate ability to apply intuition and tap into the energy of the universe, using it as a tool to create the lives we are meant to live. It is as natural to us as eating, breathing, touch, and sound. It is integral to the way we think, act, and feel. There is nowhere we have to go to get it: It is part of us.

And at this very point in time, you and I are sitting atop a kind of "psychic wormhole"—much like the one that opened to our parents three decades ago. Our parents experienced one sort of energy, but the energy that has opened to us is very different. As natural-born psychic receptors, we find that tapping into this new energy is the easiest thing in the world. And now is the time for us to claim it and use it to find out who we are.

Let me guess. You're just a little skeptical. Well, sometimes the most obvious things are the hardest to see. Besides, it's in our nature to be doubtful. We are independent thinkers, many of us are entrepreneurs, we hate rules, and because of all that we are quick to reject anything that smacks of our parents' reality.

But trust me: I've been psychic since I was three years old. Waiting for the bus to take me to nursery school one morning, I innocently said to my mother, "Don't worry, Mommy, the bus is going to be late today because the driver broke her arm last night." Sure enough, the bus showed up late, with a substitute driver at the wheel. Miss Mary indeed had a broken arm.

Needless to say, my parents freaked out.

As a member of Generation X, I'm the youngest nationally recognized psychic in America. And I can see it plain as daylight. We are brimming with spiritual abilities, and we don't have to closet ourselves in Zen monasteries or become meditative recluses in order to access them. Today, people can be both psychic and normal. Psychic energy belongs to everyone, not just monks and gurus.

I'm living proof. I grew up watching my mother meditate and do yoga. I didn't know what that stuff was all about, but I quickly formed an opinion that her activities were nebbishy hobbies mothers did in their spare time. Then, in high school, I became interested in psychic teachings. I went to the local library and took out books on palm reading, handwriting, and psychic development. They were long-winded, boring, and extremely esoteric. They didn't talk to me.

None of the spiritual teachings to which I had access seemed natural or accessible. I was disappointed. I wanted to participate, but I knew I was different. It seemed there was no way to connect these stuffy teachings with my everyday reality. The available books all implied that psychic ability was some foreign skill you had to jump through hoops to obtain. They claimed it took years of practice to develop psychic skills, and long, drawn-out rituals were needed in order to arrive at your spiritual destination. Nobody said, "Here, this is a normal and natural ability. You can be who you are and still be psychic."

It took me years to figure out what was going on. The spiritual energy our parents tapped into was hard to reach and difficult to understand. It spoke in fragments and symbols and was not easily integrated into daily experience. It took long, drawn-out rituals to receive psychic information, and those rituals were no guarantee you'd understand the information once it came to you. Those who wished to master psychic wisdom had to devote themselves entirely to attaining spiritual awareness.

On the other hand, there I was, wired completely differently—like the rest of my generation, preprogrammed with innate psychic ability and a different way of operating in the world. My experience with psychic energy has been utterly new. I've found that the closer you live to your connection, the less ritual it takes to get there. The old energy says, *Climb through a window.* Today's energy says, *Why climb through a window when you can walk through a door?*

Psychic energy and spirituality is no longer arduous to access and difficult to use in everyday life. I practice a spirituality that fits into my crammed, jet-setting lifestyle. I call it "instant gratification intuition." Let's face it, I don't think anyone in our generation would put effort into something that isn't direct, practical, and accessible. We don't have time for ambiguous symbols and hindsight; that certainly isn't going to help us get through today. We want psychic and spiritual energy in our lives, but we are hesitant. Psychic and spiritual energy has never before fit into a normal life.

The ability you're about to access, however, is as natural and normal as seeing, hearing, smelling, and touching. Right now, we take for granted that we have five senses. We get up, open our eyes, put our feet on a solid floor, hear the coffee brewing. This book will show you how to just as easily take for granted that your sixth sense is constantly perceiving, too. First you'll discover how to access the psychic abilities you already have. Then I'll show you how to deepen and broaden your psychic skills so that you can make magic and ease happen in your life—in every area from your love life to your career to a simple trip to the mall.

Tapping into your abilities is far easier and more natural than you would ever expect; it is simply a matter of working through a series of exercises, including creating a sacred space, breath work, and visualizations. Don't worry, I won't have you floating around in the lotus position or having séances while standing on your head chanting. You won't lose yourself, you won't become wacky, you won't become anything other than more of who you want to be. I promise.

Once you've gotten a sense of what psychic energy is, what your abilities are, and how to control them, in part II of this book you'll put it all to use. Many people buy into the myth that in order to achieve balance, you have to live without worldly possessions and give up your personal desires. That's boring! Living within the new energy is about manifesting yourself fully. It means living with grace: having more patience at the checkout counter, or better yet, miraculously attracting a counter with no line. It doesn't mean giving up your passion for shoes!

Opening up to the new energy around you is like using a new tool to create the life you always wanted. It will help you shed your fears and reach for your true destiny; it will lead you in the right direction; and it will help you learn life's lessons with grace and ease—even send you your soulmate.

This new energy is active. As receptors of this energy, we can pull it down, focus it, and mold it to create what we want to be. We can use it to clear obstacles in the way of our happiness and fulfillment. We can use it to help others and help our world. Think about it: If this energy force can keep nine planets in line, it can show us what we are looking for!

This book will show you, step by step, how to access this energy. You'll learn how to tune it in and how to shut it off. You'll gain the ability to focus and mold it. When you are adept at this, you can do just about anything. You can find your soulmate; discover solutions to your nagging problems; heal your aches and pains; even communicate with your spirit guides and angels. You can avoid bad relationships; prepare for meetings armed with the foreknowledge of what is going to unfold; and know when and what people are thinking about you. If nothing else, developing your psychic ability will make you popular at parties. People will be drawn to you without quite knowing why.

This book is your millennium handbook. It is an exercise program for your mind and soul. It is the most direct way to discover your own power station, and by the time you're finished, you'll be a different person. Using this energy has changed my life, for sure. I used to be on autopilot. I was unhappy; I was twenty pounds overweight; and I was afraid my future was full of failure. Once universal energy flowed through my life, I found my destiny; I lost the twenty pounds; and I now appreciate myself in a way I never thought could be.

Tapping into psychic energy puts you in a deep state of awareness that is more relaxed than the best massage or the deepest bubble bath. This book will help you get to that place easily and effortlessly. You will be able to focus on it at the drop of a hat. You will be able to get answers that will make your life easier. You will naturally become more stable and have a more grounded way of looking at the world.

And you'll need these skills. Over the next ten years, our world will undergo expansive and sweeping changes. We'll see political, social, and economic developments; earth changes; environmental, techno-logical, and energy advances. We'll need this new energy to prepare for all these global changes, and to make our own very personal definitions of success come true.

The things our parents took for granted are no longer afforded us; security is no longer available in the form of a three-bedroom house and a retirement-path job. And we wouldn't want that anyway. We want to experience our individual freedom, happiness, and destiny. Working at the same company for twenty years and living a stable life isn't good enough anymore. We seek our unique paths, the deeper meaning of why we're here. As never before, we want to recognize who we are; we want to fulfill our unique destinies. We want to go for it and not stop till we get there.

Healthy intuition and a deep understanding of "the way things work" is our natural state of grace. It is our birthright; all we have to do is rediscover it. Now more than ever, a little effort goes a long way. Come with me, and watch a new and exciting world open up right in front of you!

part one

hello,
karma
calling!

—

chapter one

how psychic
are you?

▬▬▬

Every time I'm at a party, people come up to me and say, "Oh, you're a psychic! I had this experience once; it was the weirdest thing; let me tell you *all* about it . . . blah, blah, blah . . ." They go on to tell me about a dream, a coincidence, a meeting with an angel, whatever. I have heard countless similar stories from believers and nonbelievers alike. After years of hearing these personal accounts, I am confident in saying that *everyone* has had at least one psychic experience—whether they know it or not.

Think about your own history. Have unexplainable events happened to you? Have you had a particularly powerful dream? An unusual coincidence? Then you have experienced psychic energy.

We all have psychic experiences every day. Our sixth sense is constantly working. The problem is that most of the time it is working quietly, unconsciously, and we don't even know it. Only once in a while, when perceptions pop into our conscious reality, do we identify them as psychic experiences. For example, when I first met my friend Maria, she told me that every night when she goes to sleep, she feels as though she is flying through the stars. She sees them whooshing past her at incredible speeds. She never thought much about this until a psychic explained to her that she was having out-of-body experiences—her consciousness was leaving her body when she slept and roaming around the universe. Isn't that cool? To be so naturally psychic, and have no idea of it!!

Identifying these events and experiences in your own life is the first step toward awakening your psychic abilities. Recognizing the process that is already going on in your head is the key to understanding what psychic energy looks like and feels like, and how it's already a big force in your life.

Psychic energy is supercharged energy. When you connect with it, it sends a chill down your spine or creates a tingle on your skin. Being in the flow of this energy is like catching a buzz without having a drink. It is a warm, energizing feeling. The longer you are in contact with it, the deeper your connection gets. After a while, you feel like you are floating.

Professional psychics know how to connect to this energy at will and let it flow through their bodies. They are so comfortable with the energy that feeling supercharged is second nature to them. Psychics are the universe's weightlifters: They are accustomed to using their bodies to connect and channel this energy so they can carry a heavy spiritual load without feeling overwhelmed. Once when I was doing readings at a client's party, I was there for five hours, completely in this zone. People told me that when they came near me I was emanating so much energy the hair on the back of their necks stood up.

There are many ways to access the energy of the universe. You can do it through physical exercise such as yoga, tai chi, or tae kwon do. You can access it through meditation, or by using psychic tools and sciences such as tarot cards, crystals, rune stones, the I Ching, astrology, numerology, or Ouija boards. All these tools and techniques are disciplines that integrate the body, mind, and spirit to enable us to enter into a psychic mode. You may have played with some of these in the past. In this book I will show you how to cultive your natural internal connection to psychic energy and get the answers you want without using any of these tools. Once you understand how to connect to psychic energy, you can study and use one of the disciplines that I just mentioned—as many professional psychics do—but I'll leave that for someone else's book!

Some people are more naturally aware of this energy, with or without discipline training. Dreams, coincidences, hearing or seeing something otherworldly, even experiencing a deep knowing feeling about something are rare, spontaneous psychic experiences that form the foundation of your budding psychic ability. You suddenly think about a long-lost friend who miraculously calls a few hours later. You have a dream about a fishing trip and then you're suddenly invited on one. In a scary situation, you feel a calming presence nearby. You feel the need to walk on a certain side of the road for no apparent reason, then the next day you hear about a building collapse that narrowly missed you. These events are valid psychic experiences.

Many people are aware that they have had spontaneous psychic experiences in the past, but they don't know what to do with them. They treat them like the bearded lady at the circus. Gawking at your psychic experiences is not the way to go. These events are messages. They are here to tell you something. By oohing and ahhing at them, you keep them at a distance. In order to develop your psychic ability, you must use these spontaneous psychic experiences to the fullest. Start by recognizing them, not judging them, hiding them, or gawking at them.

Your spontaneous experiences will probably fall into one of several categories: déjà vu, coincidences, dreams, and knowing feelings. You may also feel chills after hearing, seeing, or thinking something. Let's look into these different points of contact for a moment.

Some people frequently experience déjà vu, that ten-second feeling of having been somewhere or done something before. You know exactly what's going to happen next. Coincidences are extremely common; meaningful coincidence is what psychoanalyst Carl Jung termed synchronicity. Let's say you go on a job interview, and you find that the person in charge of hiring went to the same school you did—and had the same teachers. On your way to meet a friend you get lost, only to find yourself in front of a store that sells that tiny, perfect kitchen table you've been so desperately seeking.

Coincidences happen constantly—and they keep happening over and over until we finally get the message. How many times do you need to hear people talk about nurses, how many advertisements and commercials for hospitals or nursing schools do you need to see—before it finally dawns on you that you should go back to school to become a nurse? Synchronicities usually point us in a direction or validate the direction we are already going in. The most important thing to remember is that they are supposed to get your attention—so listen up!

People who refuse to use their psychic abilities during their waking hours often experience predictive dreams. It's got to come out somewhere! You may dream that you are sitting at a clean new desk and the next day get a call from a headhunter offering you a job. You may dream that your sister is pregnant, and the following month she tells you the important news. Recognizing these dreams is difficult; we often ignore them or forget them as soon as we get up. Learning how to recognize them and pay attention to them can give you a glimpse into the future.

Getting chills down your spine or a tingle in your skin does not always mean you are cold. These are sure-fire signs that you have connected to the universal energy. You may not realize this, but chills are often a reaction to having a specific thought or seeing or hearing something. The instant you connect to psychic energy, it feels like putting a sixty-watt bulb into a forty-watt socket. Chills and tingles are your body's way of saying, "*Wow!* That's a lot of energy!"

Has something like this ever happened? You are joking around with a friend and you say, "All I want is a new car!" You get chills. I bet that sometime soon you will get that new car. You may see a terrible traffic jam on the news and think, "I hope my mom isn't stuck in that." And you feel a tingle on your skin. I bet your mom somehow got right into that traffic!

These experiences constantly happen to me and my friends. We can't have a conversation without finishing each other's sentences. When we get together, there are two common phrases flying around the room. One is "I was just going to say that" and the other is "Get outta my head!"

Now, stop here. Before you read on, grab a pen and paper and examine your personal psychic history. Chances are, you haven't forgotten your own psychic experiences. Most people remember the biggies for a long time. Write down every experience you have had that resembles what you've been reading about in these pages. Dreams, coincidences, feelings, odd events: Once you have them in writing, you will begin to see how psychic you really have been over the years.

There are different types of psychic abilities, and it's likely that you are most gifted in one or two of these. In the following chapters, you are not only going to learn to have more psychic experiences, you are also going to learn how to become stronger in the area you're naturally gifted in. As you develop that ability, you will continue to process information through the same channels and methods that your brain has been using all along.

The first step is to find out what kind of natural psychic you are. As you read these definitions, go back to your list of previous spontaneous psychic experiences and see what group they fall under. Once you identify the one or two receptors that are naturally yours, you will be able to understand them and use them more effectively.

We all have *all* these psychic senses. You may have an affinity for one of these abilities over the others for many reasons. You may be more comfortable receiving information in a certain manner. You may be completely adept at processing information through visual psychic images, but maybe the idea of hearing a bump in the night sends you reeling. The universe knows this stuff and is not in the business of terrifying anyone. If you have an aversion to any of these abilities, don't worry; your natural receptor isn't all of a sudden going to change after you read this.

Clairvoyance. This is literally being able to see events occurring with your inner sight, also known as your third eye or mind's eye. When you close your eyes, do you naturally see visually or photographically? If so, you have a natural affinity for this type of psychic ability.

Clairsentience. The least-used and the most commonly noted ability among psychics and nonpsychics alike. Sentience means to feel something. Have you ever just *known* something, with all your being, and not been able to come up with exactly where you got that piece of information?

Clairaudience. This means you hear things. People who have active clairaudient abilities are able to hear angels, spirit guides, and messages from the universe. They tend to have a specific place in their heads where they receive these messages—like a spot in the middle of the head, behind their ears, or on the forehead (the third-eye area).

Telepathy. This is a fun one! Telepathy is sending and receiving thoughts and messages. This usually happens with people with whom you are strongly connected, such as friends and family. When the phone rings, do you know it's your best friend calling? Think about this—it's quicker for you to receive a thought than it is for the sender to pick up the phone and dial your number.

Precognition. The abilities I have listed so far all happen, by definition, in real time; that is, at the same time they are occurring. (Some people use the term *clairvoyant* to describe future sight, but that's a matter of interpretation.) Being precognitive is having the ability to sense an event before it occurs. This information can be received through a deep knowing, a precognitive dream, or the use of tools and techniques like the tarot cards or the I Ching.

For the next two weeks, keep a psychic record. Have a notebook close to you whenever possible. Go about your daily activities but whenever you experience a coincidence, an odd event, or a dream, write it down. I suggest you go so far as to keep a pen and paper in bed with you to immediately record your dreams. This is not as crazy as it sounds, as long as you get over the initial shock of sleeping with a notebook! I keep a notebook in my bed, and it has been an invaluable tool for my psychic ability and my creativity as well.

Although I have a tendency to go all out, don't feel that you have to go nuts with this assignment. You can make a mental note of an event and write it down later or limit yourself to recording only brief descriptions. Whichever way works best for you, after two weeks I bet you'll be surprised at what you've experienced.

This is not going to be a big waste of your time, no matter how frequently or infrequently you have psychic incidents. How do I know this? I have given this assignment to many of my clients, and within weeks of carrying it out, they all reported having had the coolest experiences. One client kept having deep feelings that she was going to get a computer soon. She was seeing it with her inner vision, but she didn't trust these visuals, and told me that she kept thinking she was daydreaming. (Yeah, right!) A few weeks later, her ex-boss gave her a used computer. She was—and is—elated!

When two weeks have passed, reread all the entries you have made. You will probably find that they are concentrated in one or two of the ability groups listed. Voilà! Your natural psychic ability or abilities—simple as that. Let's say, for example, that one day you felt as though you were going to need your umbrella even though the sky was clear and sunny. What you felt was clairsentience. It was also pre-cognition. Or say that during a daydream, you visually imagined your sister's car breaking down, and later, your mother called to report that very thing. That was clairvoyance.

Once you know what channel you're psychically on, you have an idea of what ability you are going to work on developing. The next task is to get from having psychic experiences spontaneously to actu-ally *making* them happen whenever you want. You'll start with a series of exercises designed to get you into an energy-receptive state. Here are a few tools you'll need to effectively work the exercises through. Keep the following items near this book.

- *A psychic journal.* *You'll need a notebook to write everything down in so that you can gauge your progress. You've already had a taste of this with your two-week journal. By logging every experience and exer-cise—and believe me, when you start working with this energy, the coolest things will begin to happen—you will help yourself see that you are having valid psychic experiences. We are often too tough on our-selves, not trusting that what we are feeling, hearing, and seeing really does mean anything. Notebooks don't lie. If you've written it down, you cannot argue with yourself. You'll be surprised to see the amazing va-lidity that many of the feelings you used to dismiss will come to have.*

- *A pen, a highlighter, and a black marker.* *Obviously, you know what to do with the pen, so let me explain the other two. The highlighter and the marker are to help you develop your own unique relationship with this book. Not that you need to become as one with these two hundred pages, but this volume will become your channel-opener, the tool to your psychic success. I suggest you make it completely your own by freely highlighting sections of the text that will help you connect faster. Liberally cross out any sentences that get in your way. Write in the margins, between the lines, and wherever else you want.*

Actively evaluate all the exercises as you complete them. You will have natural likes and dislikes for certain ones. Enjoy it; this is probably the only time it's constructive to deface a book!

- **Time.** *I call the ability you're cultivating "instant gratification intuition," but it will take a little time for it to sprout. I suggest that you set aside thirty to forty-five scheduled minutes each week. Try three ten-to-fifteen-minute sessions, let's say on Monday, Wednesday, and Friday. Or plan two ten-minute sessions during the week with a twenty-minute session on the weekend. The goal is a consistent and comfortable schedule that works for you. Set up a routine that fits your comfort zone, because the most important thing is to enjoy spending time doing these exercises. We all know we never keep at something that's a pain-in-the-butt effort. If it means devoting just one twenty-minute block of time once a week, that's fine. You'll see progress no matter what you do.*

  There is no need to do all these exercises at once. Don't overwhelm yourself; your ability is going to develop anyway. Try each one, in order, at least once before going on. Do the exercises at your own pace. Linger on the ones you want to explore more. If you get restless during a session, wind it down. Take a week off. Trust your instincts.

- **Attitude.** *This is your exercise gear. You may be able to do the exercises without a pen, but you won't get anywhere without the right frame of mind. Decide how much you believe in your own psychic ability and your capacity for growth. Your intention is the real power behind this ability. How much freedom are you going to give yourself to experiment as you go through this book? How high or low is your resistance to change? The answers to these questions will determine your ability to develop your psychic experiences. You set the pace for your own progress. The ease with which you develop your psychic ability is directly related to your comfort with new experiences, and how much you identify with your current frame of mind. If you accept that there are many ways of being/thinking/doing, you can easily let go of any limited* *thinking that may keep you from developing your natural abilities. This will expand your thinking to include your newfound abilities.*

Now that you've got your tools, you're ready for the exercises. I call my sessions psychic workouts. They are designed to get you into an energy-receptive state and develop your psychic muscles.

During each session you will sit quietly for ten to fifteen minutes. You'll close your eyes, and then you'll progress through a series of action-oriented instructions. To the naked eye, it may seem that you are sitting doing nothing. But you will never be doing nothing. Your brain will be constantly moving from one step to the next. The end result is a well-formed psychic connection.

I don't like rules and regulations. You can do these exercises sitting up, lying down, standing on your head if you want to—you're the boss. You can do them anywhere, at any time: after work, at two o'clock in the morning, when you're at the gym or in your car, whenever. These are *your* choices, and you can be as creative as you want. Fit the exercises into your life as they fit best.

In the next chapter, you'll go through your first session and learn everything you need to do to set up the perfect psychic workout. You'll learn how to create a sacred space, say a prayer of protection, and open your connection to the universal or psychic energy. You'll learn how to shut off that link and end your session. I'll show you specific gauges that will tell you—for sure—that you made a successful connection.

Once you know how to set up a workout, you'll jump right to the starting line with a few simple exercises to let psychic energy start flowing through you. Get ready, get set, GO!!

Once you've come to your psychic senses, you will be able to:

- Connect with friends without using a telephone.
- Know when your favorite clothing designer is having a sale.
- Avoid messy traffic jams.
- Know that your boss's pen will run out—so you'll bring two to that meeting.
- Send instant messages to your significant other.
- Organize your life more intuitively and freely.
- Navigate unforeseen obstacles with aplomb.
- Do things you previously thought impossible.
- Know who is on the other end of the phone when it rings.
- Talk to your dog.
- Get the winning lottery numbers.
- Know what your mother is cooking for dinner.
- Know that your aunt is going to stop by for dessert.
- Know that she likes apple pie!

chapter two

losing your psychic virginity

———

I remember one of the recurring psychic experiences of my childhood. Asleep at night, I was constantly being waked up by different voices coming from behind my ear in the back of my head. "Pssst, Stacey. Stacey!"

Believe me, there are a lot of spirits out there who love an audience when they know they can be heard. To get to sleep, I had to sit up in bed and explain to them that I didn't want to hear them anymore. Can you imagine—a seven-year-old reasoning with something that isn't entirely there? And to make doubly sure I didn't hear the spirit voices, I slept with the covers over my ears—as if that was going to block out something coming from inside my head!

I didn't tell my parents about this until just recently. Their response was, "Why didn't you tell us?" Yeah, that would've gone over well. Besides, I really thought everyone heard voices in the back of their heads. Losing your psychic virginity—it's a funny thing. Everyone has a first experience that they don't know what to do with and can't quite explain. These events are, collectively, the first step to becoming psychically savvy. I think my life would be so boring without these way-out happenings. But now that you've read about my first experience, don't all of a sudden get scared. Something as shocking and wacky as my nightly voice parades probably won't happen to you on your first try.

Your First Psychic Experience

In the last chapter, you got a sense of the spontaneous psychic experiences you've been having all your life, and you figured out what type of experiences they were. Now you are ready to have your first consciously created psychic experience. To create a solid and enjoyable first experience, there are a series of steps that you are going to go through. For now, just get these down and do them the right way. You can worry about actually picking up on the psychic energy later on in this chapter.

The first thing you'll do is create a sacred space. This will help you get out of the ordinary energy that surrounds you now and create a space big enough to tune into the psychic energy all around you. Next, you'll say a prayer of protection to balance your inner energy and help you release anything that might get in the way of the perfect psychic experience.

These are ritual-like steps designed to get you into the psychic flow and open the connection to your psychic source. Once you've felt what it is like to be in the flow, you will close your connection and end your session. Afterward, it's important that you write about the experience in your journal so you can chart your development. From now on, the last step in all your psychic workouts will be this journal writing.

These steps—creating your sacred space, saying the prayer of protection, getting into a flow, ending your session, and writing in your

10 Best Ways to Lose Your Psychic Virginity

One You dream that Arnold Schwarzenegger wants to come over on a motorcycle and take you on a ride into the fourth dimension.

Two You have an out-of-body experience and end up in the kitchen eating a box of chocolate chip cookies—a no-calorie snack!

Three You see fairies and angels for the first time and they are doing the macarena.

Four Trying to do a thousand situps, you accidentally levitate up to the ceiling.

Five You are meditating in the park, and a passerby tries to give you a dollar.

Six You try to call your mother, and Dionne Warwick answers the phone.

Seven You're daydreaming, and Houdini shows up with tomorrow's winning lottery numbers.

Eight You're talking to your dog. He starts talking back.

Nine You meet your spirit guide for the first time, and he sounds exactly like Elmer Fudd.

Ten Captain Kirk interrupts one of your dreams, shouting, "C'mon, we're going where no man has gone before . . . and we're late!"

journal—are the essentials for a proper psychic development. They make up a complete first experience, and they become your way to access psychic energy from now on. You'll be doing them over and over, each time you do a psychic workout session, and by the end of this chapter they'll become second nature, like the rituals you do getting ready for work: get out of bed, take a shower, make some coffee, get dressed, watch *Good Morning America*. Once you have a working understanding of all the steps, you'll integrate them into every psychic workout you do from now on.

Creating a Sacred Space

Whether they realize it or not, people create sacred spaces all the time. When cooking a romantic dinner for two, what's the first thing you do? Light candles and put on mood music. You do this not only because it looks good but because it creates a certain energy.

We start every psychic session by creating a sacred space. When first starting out, it is important to create a physical and mental arena in which it is safe to learn and grow. This place offers supportive energy for the exercises you'll be doing. It is a place to be honest with yourself—a place to create miracles and transformations in your life.

No matter where we are in our psychic development, we are always learning and growing; often we are working through negative patterns. In a sacred space, we suspend any negativity, doubt, or fear that might hamper our growth while we are doing our psychic workouts.

To begin, you will need to gather up some sacred space items. First, buy some candles. You can use as many as you want, in whatever color. I prefer white candles because they resonate all colors at once. (Remember that from eighth-grade science? In case you don't—white light through a prism breaks into a rainbow.) White reminds me of angel wings.

If you prefer another color, here is a description of what other colors mean so you know what you are getting into:

Yellow or gold—future success and clarity
Pink—love
Orange—stability
Green—healing and nurturing
Blue—calming and communication
Purple—intuition and psychic ability (not a bad color for this work)

You may want to buy candles of several colors and use them for the different exercises. Try a green or blue candle for Relaxing with Universal Energy (page 37) or an orange candle for Grounding (page 39).

The one color I left out on purpose is red. Red is passionate, but it can also be aggressive. If I need energy, I use orange; it has all the energy-boosting qualities of red without negative side effects. And don't forget, this is your sacred space. If you don't like candles, don't use 'em.

Candle Me!

Here's how to take ordinary grocery store candles and make them powerful and personal. Rub or spray your favorite oil, scent, or perfume on the length of a candle (almond or vanilla extract works, even squeezing a fresh lemon or orange). As the candle burns down, the oil will be released into the air, filling your sacred space with your favorite scent. If the candle is already lit, drop some of the scent into the melted wax near the flame. Don't put it on the wick, or it might not light. And don't spray perfume directly onto the flame—this is not pyrotechnic school.

Next, gather up some belongings that are important to you. These can be incense, angel figurines, shells, photographs, a rock from your favorite mountain, an autographed ticket stub—anything that is special to you. If you want to go all the way, find a perfect box to keep them in—a crate, a basket, a decorated shoebox. These items are powerful energy reminders, and they should be kept in a safe place until you bring them out for every psychic session.

With your special items in hand, choose the location of your sacred space. This can be anywhere you feel comfortable: your kitchen, your living room, your bedroom, even the attic or the backyard. Then set up your candles and your items. There are a few ways you can do this. You can line them up in front of you on a table, the floor, or a shelf to create an altar. You also can place the items around you in the shape of a circle, square, or triangle.

These particular shapes have meanings, too. A square creates four points. To me that signifies grounding: a solid foundation. A triangle represents a pyramid with three energy points, indicating the alignment of body, mind, and soul. If you sit in a triangle facing one of the points, it connects to spirit; if the point is behind you, it is a connection to the physical world. A circle—with no beginning and no end—signifies unity.

Now you are ready to say a prayer for your sacred space. No, this didn't suddenly turn into Sunday school! Prayers and powerful words invoke a certain energy within us. When you say something with intention, it is so. Personally, I think of this activity as a prayer, but I also call it an "invocation," a more universal term.

I like prayers and invocations that are traditional. Again, I personally think of God when I am calling on a higher source, because it makes me feel a deep connection to what created me and what I am a part of. But if this is sticky for you, use "Spirit," as I have indicated. Feel free to rearrange these words and speak them to anyone and anything you feel connected to. That's what your pen is for!

Light the candles as you say these words.

Invocation for Creating a Sacred Space
Dear Spirit,
As I light these candles, bless this sacred place.
Let the light of their flames radiate love and protection to all four corners
of this room.
I ask at this time that any negative energies be released from this space.
With a bath of white light, I ask that it be cleansed and neutralized.
Turn my dwelling into a sanctuary.
May it be the foundation for your teachings and the inspiration for my
higher perceptions.
Amen.

Reciting this should take less than a minute.

Open your eyes and look around. You now have a sacred space! You will know that you have reached that space when you see your surroundings a bit differently. This is subtle. Things will appear crisp, energized, glowing. You may get a chill up your spine or on the back of your neck.

When you feel a deep sense of peace, you are ready to begin. Don't worry if you don't feel this at first; pretend you're in a Nike commercial and just do it. You'll start feeling it as you become more sensitive to psychic energy.

Portable Sacred Space

You can do your psychic workouts at the beach, on a hike, or in a hotel room. Here's how. First, create sacred space items from things you see around you that are special to that place: sea shells, fallen leaves . . . you can even rip out pictures of the local scenes from the brochures in the hotel lobby. Place them around you, and go on with your psychic workout as you normally would. Voilà!

Instant Sacred Space

Don't have time to create a sacred space? Try working with just one candle. Light it while reciting the prayer for sacred space. Thirty seconds and you're on your way. No excuses!

Protect Yourself

We've all heard horror stories about Ouija board sessions. Young people think it's a *game*! They play with their older sister's board when she's not at home or do it while drinking beer at college parties. Without knowing any better, people just sit down and say, "Hey, anyone want to come talk to us?" It seems harmless at first, until they get some negative entity that tells them it is the Devil and starts spewing out negative sentiments. This can scare the daylights out of anyone. There's an easy thing you can do to prevent this from ever happening to you: After you create a sacred space, be sure to say an invocation of protection. It's extra important to say a brief invocation before doing any psychic work in order to put yourself in a positive, pure, and balanced state.

This is the key to having really great psychic experiences. And this is why Ouija boards get such a bad rap. Sitting down and saying, "Hey, anyone want to come talk to us?" is the wrong thing to do! You need to clear yourself of any negativity and only talk to your spirit guides and your angels. Just because a spirit isn't in a body doesn't mean it has your best interests at heart. Don't ever—in any of your psychic roamings— open up and just talk to anything or anybody. That is like opening your door to strangers. You just wouldn't do it.

Your invocation of protection is a way of surrounding yourself with the highest form of love, and releasing your own negativity as well as all negative energy surrounding you. This will ensure that you receive information only from the most pure sources. Say the following words each time you make a connection to psychic or universal energy:

Invocation of Protection
Dear Spirit,
As I sit with you now, I open my heart.
I surround myself with the love and light of your protection.
I release any negativity that I have picked up throughout the day so that
    I speak to the universe with the purity of my soul.
I ask that any energy (information, healing) be given for my absolute
    good.
Dismiss now all energies that are not of the Highest and Greatest source.
As I bathe in your grace, I will listen to your resounding voice within me.
I will be true to my heart and your gentle guidance.
Amen.

I usually follow this invocation with a moment of appreciation. The universe loves to be appreciated; saying thank you is our gift back. A moment of thanks will double the good stuff coming your way:

Thank you for all the goodness and abundance in my life.

You can be even more specific and list friends, family, your job, anything for which you are thankful.

I love this part: Every time I thank the universe, I get a huge *chill* all over—and I feel like I've stuck my finger in an electric socket. Great analogy, huh? Well, I know it's working!

Opening Up and Going with the Flow
Getting into a Basic Receptive State

OK, time for the main course. Now that you have created and protected your sacred space, you are ready to turn on the flow of psychic
energy. You'll start with a basic receptive, meditative state.

I know what you're thinking. "No, not meditation!" A few years
ago I was scared of meditation, too. When I first studied the psychic
senses, meditation kept coming up over and over again. My initial
reaction was to reject it as restrictive and boring. I have so much energy, I can't sit still. I can't meditate, I thought. My *mother* used to
meditate!

I remember she took a course at our local library. The class sat
silently in a room and when everyone graduated, they each got their
own secret word. This made no sense to me back then (and, I admit, it
still doesn't). I realized, however, that I didn't have to do things just as
my mother did. I don't like to meditate, in the dry sense of the word.
I like having the freedom to itch and twitch if I want to.

Unfortunately, there is no better word than "meditation" to describe the practice of getting into an open and receptive state. But my
psychic workout sessions are action meditations. Follow the instructions and go with it; despite the lingo, I promise it will be an enjoyable
experience.

Here is the quickie version of what you're going to do. You'll sit
down in your sacred space, close your eyes, quiet your mind, and focus
on breathing deeply. It is very important that you take a few minutes
and get it right, since this quieting of your mind is the basis for all the
exercises in the book. It is the first thing you have to master before you
can get down and dirty with psychic energy and create the life you
want.

There is no special position you need to be in, though personally I
prefer sitting up with my legs crossed on the couch. You can position
yourself in a comfortable chair with your feet flat on the floor; you can

flop on the floor with your feet on a chair—I don't care, as long as you're comfortable. Sometimes I have so much energy that I can't sit down, so I get into my receptive state while standing up with my arms outstretched as far apart as they'll go. To me, that position says, "Here I am, Universe, I am ready! Let's go!"

As you breathe, feel the energy electrify your body. Awaken your inner self and listen from within. Feel your belly rise and fall; hear the air moving through your nostrils. Concentrate on the inner experience. Every breath is nourishment for your body and soul.

When you have a sense of electricity and heightened inner senses, you have made it. You should feel a change within two or three breaths. Wasn't it easy?!

OK. Once you're in this expanded state, stay there for a few moments and enjoy it. You'll be using this deep state of awareness as a springboard for the exercises in later chapters, so two or three minutes should do it.

AT A GLANCE
Getting into a Basic Receptive State

Step One In a comfortable position, close your eyes.

Step Two Quiet your mind by focusing on your breathing.

Step Three Breathe deeply. Take slow, deep, full breaths from your belly.

Step Four Concentrate on the flow of electric energy, the pulse of your breath. You are inviting the universal, psychic energy into your life. Let it flow through you. Relax into it and let go.

If you feel like you don't quite understand how this process works, or if you are a little confused, give yourself a break. It will be easier the second time you try it, and by your third time it becomes old hat. And don't worry if you're fidgety or if your mind is racing. That will stop when you get the hang of it—which shouldn't take too long, because, don't forget, you are a natural-born psychic.

Put Your Psychic Abilities to the Test!

The next time you are doing a psychic workout, get into a deep receptive state and ask yourself a few questions. As you breathe deeply with your eyes closed, concentrate on your eyes and forehead with your inner senses. Pick a friend or family member (only pick one who is supportive of this psychic stuff, or you'll freak 'em out). First, ask yourself what that person is doing right now, then ask yourself what will happen with that person this week. Do you see pictures, shapes, or colors? Then you have active clairvoyance. Don't forget to write down the answers you receive and check with that person. If you got correct impressions to the first question, then that may also be considered telepathy. If you got correct answers to the second, it is precognition.

Close your eyes again and breathe deeply. Concentrate on your hearing with your inner senses. Again, focus on a friend or family member. Ask yourself what that person is doing right now, then ask yourself what will happen with that person this week. Do you hear words or sounds from outside your ear or inside your head? That is active clairaudience. Write down the answers when you are finished and check their accuracy. Correct impressions about the first question may be telepathic. Correct answers to the second may be precognitive.

Close your eyes and get into a deep state one more time. Focus your attention only on the first question this time instead of on your inner eyes or inner ears. What is that friend doing right now? Begin to answer the question with your *knowing* mind. What do you feel or sense? Write or say anything that comes up. Go on to the next question, What will happen with this person this week? If you get any impressions by *just knowing* them, then you have active clairsentience. Again, the knowledge about the first question is telepathic; about the second, it is precognitive.

Closing Your Sacred Space

Congratulations! You've just had your first planned psychic experience. You've been psychically deflowered! Now you just have to end your session correctly.

All my psychic workouts have a distinct closing element to them, whether it's spinning a cocoon of white light around yourself, putting a shield of protection around yourself, or pulling psychic energy around you in a protective bubble. These are all ways to shut off the energy flow you just accessed, in order to close your connection.

If you don't turn off the faucet after you brush your teeth, you'll eventually have a flood on your hands. Likewise, if you leave your psychic connection open, impressions will seep in throughout the day and you will not be able to function. I certainly wouldn't be able to concentrate on the physical world around me if I was constantly feeling things, hearing things, and seeing things with my inner senses.

When people first meet me they often ask me if I am sensing things all day long. No. I decided long ago that when I am *in*, I'm in, and when I'm *out*, I'm out. *In* means I am in a receptive state; that is where I get information. I have a hard time being logical when I am in. *Out* means I am functioning in the outside world and am unavailable—for the most part—to the other side. Important things still get through, and I can easily touch base for inner guidance so I don't miss anything. But I don't consciously receive in the out mode.

This is probably the way you'll work best. You'll go in for psychic sessions, and you will be in receiving mode. When you are finished and have closed your session, you will be back to operating in normal *out* mode. When you get better at this you will see how easy it is to touch base with your inner guidance systems, and you will be able to flick your psychic on/off switch whenever you wish.

Turning the switch to off is easy. If you say something with intention—it is so. I end my sessions by simply closing my sacred space. For this I use another simple invocation.

Invocation for Closing Your Connection and Your Sacred Space
Dear Spirit,
Thank you for sharing this sacred time with me.
I appreciate the flow of energy I have just experienced.

I will use it for my Highest good.
As I blow out these candles, I close this sacred space, and I ask that your
    protection surround me wherever I go today.
Amen.

Feel free to close your sessions in a different way, if you'd like. Visualize a stop sign or visualize a light bulb going out. Visualize yourself talking on an inner telephone. When you're done—hang up. Or just say, "I'm finished, and will no longer be open to this energy. Poof! Over with!" As long as what you do or say has a disconnecting quality, it will work great.

Last but Not Least: Your Psychic Journal . . .

Now that you have finished your first psychic workout, what did you think of it? Was it enjoyable? Powerful? Boring? Did you experience anything unusual or extraordinary? Now is the time to take out your journal and expound with abandon. Write down your specific impressions and what you want to remember for your next workouts.

This writing is important for measuring your progress. Every detail is significant. The more you write, the more you'll connect your inner senses to your outer perceptions. You'll realize how good you are at what you're doing. And it will inspire you to go on, and on, and on, and on!

Had a Hard Time Letting Go? Don't Let That Skeptical Side Get the Best of You . . .

If you didn't truly catch a psychic buzz from the last series of ritual exercises, you may have been holding onto fear, doubt, or negativity that prevented you from making a clear energy connection. Here's what you skittish types need to do in order to suspend that doubt and get some good work done. The goal is to create a detached environment so you can get outside yourself and beyond what is blocking you.

First, get used to the idea of letting go. Your inner voice may be saying, "This isn't going to work. She says we're all psychic—I don't believe it. Not me." You can believe whatever you want, as long as you try this: Set aside a short block of time, say, twenty minutes on a Thursday evening. Schedule it for the end of the week, so you have plenty of time beforehand to get used to the idea that you will be doing a successful psychic workout.

Then tell yourself, "OK. Even though this seems crazy, I'm going to play along. Next Thursday, I am giving myself twenty minutes to go with the flow, give it a shot, and see what happens." Remind yourself of this every day until Thursday.

On the appointed time, set up your sacred space and go about your session as I described earlier. When you say your protection prayer, add these words:

Invocation of Detachment
*I release all negativity that may be buried deep within my soul interfering with
me having this transcending experience.*
*For the next twenty minutes, I suspend any disbelief, doubt, and fear that may be
limiting my development.*
*With these words, eliminate all energies that are not operating from the highest
sources.*
Amen.

Take a few deep breaths to help get yourself into a receptive place. Breathe in the expansive and unlimiting psychic energy. As you breathe out, release fear and doubt. You will know that you have made a connection and surmounted your doubts when you open your eyes and feel an odd sense of peace, and a knowing-ness you can't quite pinpoint.

Everyone has this ability—*everyone*. So if you don't feel anything at first, know that every effort you put in is adding up to that one huge moment when you have your first conscious psychic experience. When it happens, you will breathe a sigh of relief and say, "Ah-hah!"

Moving to More Structured Psychic Experiences

A few minutes ago, you had a bona fide connection with psychic energy. You saw for yourself how natural and simple the whole thing was. You realized that you can control your psychic destiny. Wasn't it easier than you thought it was going to be?

Now you're going to build on that success by moving on to some exercises that show you how to manipulate and play around with psychic energy. The first exercise, Relaxing with Universal Energy, teaches you to focus the energy and to use it to calm yourself. The second exercise, Grounding, involves sending energy whooshing through your body—up and down and in and out, as if you are part of an electric cord. The third exercise, In and Up, takes your inner senses on an inner journey. The fourth exercise, Inner Listening, explores how to discern the world with your inner senses and flex the psychic muscles I talked about in chapter 1, such as clairvoyance, clairaudience, and clairsen-tience.

I suggest you spend a week or two playing around with these exer-cises before moving on to chapter 3. If you like any of these workouts, you can keep doing them. Include them in your schedule as you move through this book.

For all these exercises, begin by using the sacred space, invocation

You Want Psychic Proof? Don't Be Surprised If . . .

. . . sacred space candle flames go nuts during your workouts! Don't worry if they start talking to you this way. Flames may flicker really fast for long periods of time, burn tremendous amounts of smoke, get really long and thin, or get really flat and wide. This is how you'll know when you are really getting into it. The flame is saying, "Yes! Yes! Yes!" Sometimes I see a golden vapor surrounding the flame that's so thick I can hardly see through it. I know my spirit guides so well that I can tell what spirit is around by looking at the flame.

. . . time seems distorted! Here's a concept for you: Time was created by the universe for us so that as we learn and grow, not everything happens at once. My guides put it this way: "One could not savor the moment, enjoying individual victories, if there was no time." I'm not here to philosophize, but somehow when you get into a deep state, you bypass the rigidity of time. It can slow down or speed up. You may find that your sessions seem to last forever, when only ten minutes have gone by, or you may feel that only moments have gone by, when the clock tells you it's been a half-hour. When you're in the flow, time is a psychic tool at your disposal. Rev it up!

. . . you see flashes of light out of the corners of your eyes. Peripheral vision is a great thing. If you are going to see lights or other visual phenomena, it's more likely that you'll see them out of the corner of your eye than straight on. One of my psychic friends was walking down the street and saw a flash coming toward her so bright that she thought she was about to bump into another person. The feeling was so strong, she instinctively jumped out of the way—of nothing! The people on the street thought she was nuts.

. . . you see signs. Coincidences, coincidences, coincidences. The more sessions you do, the more the universe will talk to you. This is true: During one relationship long ago, I noticed the not-very-common last name of my boyfriend everywhere—in books, magazines, TV commercials. While riding a bus, I looked up randomly and saw a building with his last name on it—and to top it off, the building's number was 666! Needless to say, the relationship wasn't long-lived, and it wasn't pretty. I can laugh now, but I can't say I wasn't warned.

. . . something gets misplaced. Spirit guides and angels enjoy a good joke, just like the rest of us. They have highly developed senses of humor, and a lot of time on their hands. If you swear you put your keys down in a certain place and then can't find them anywhere, or if you absolutely know you hung that mirror horizontally and it is now vertical—this is not your imagination. Look for the message behind the movement!

. . . you feel someone is standing in an empty room or you think you're hearing voices when nobody is around. Don't worry, you have not become schizophrenic. The skills that were once a part of your subconscious are now conscious. As you go about your day, especially when you are alone in a quiet place, you may be picking up psychic vibes. This happens to me all the time. Once I saw a cat jump out of an empty paper bag on my kitchen floor. I don't own a cat.

If you have one of these experiences, you can just take it as another manifestation of your budding ability, or you can get more information on it during one of your psychic sessions. But don't stop!

. . . smoke starts to form the shapes of objects. Smoke is not just smoke—it's another psychic tool. All you have to do is watch it. You can use smoke from a candle that has just been blown out, or smoke from burning incense or smudge sticks (dried sage used in rituals). Once when a friend and I blew out our sacred space candles after a session, the smoke formed an angel wing. Separately, we drew pictures of what we'd seen. The images were identical.

. . . you feel chills and changes in the air. You are sitting alone in a room with a closed window, and you suddenly feel a cool breeze or a chill up your spine. The air feels cool, dense, thick, electric. This energy is so powerful that your eyes may tear up. All I can say is . . . congratulations, you can be sure something psychic is going on.

of protection, and basic receptive state as your foundation. After you have achieved a quiet state, do the steps as instructed. When you are finished, close your sacred space and end your session by writing in your journal.

Psychic Workout
Relaxing with Universal Energy

In this workout, Dr. Universe is going to give you your very own private consultation. You are going to spend this session relaxing, so I suggest lying down flat on your back to begin. But you're the boss, so if you want to do it any other way, feel free to get creative.

As always, first create your sacred space, recite the invocation of protection, and enter a basic receptive state. Then close your eyes and visually create a ball of golden or white liquid light four or five feet above your body. It is made of pure psychic or universal energy. It doesn't have to be ball-shaped; you can make it an angel, a star, or any other form you identify with.

Visualize a cord extending from the ball of light to a comfortable place on your body, such as the top of your head, your heart, or your solar plexus. Throughout this exercise, you will use that cord to pull the universal energy toward you.

Use the light that is coming through the cord to surround yourself with a warm, protective womb or cloud. Then fill your entire body with that calming energy. Breathe deeply in and out, and feel the pulsating energy move through your body.

When you are ready, relax each part of your body in a slow wave. Start with your toes, move up through your feet, ankles, calves, knees, thighs, pelvis, hips, stomach, ribs, and chest, through the arms, elbows, hands, and fingers. Back to your shoulders, neck, jaw, eyes . . . all the way to the top of your head. Spending one deep breath on each part of your body, focus the light directly into that place. Feel the nourishing light dissolving stress there.

When you have gone through each area of your body and completed the relaxation, you can stay in this quiet place for as long as you like. Keep pulling down the light from your cord. When you are ready to end your session, use the universal energy to create a protective bubble around yourself and to dissolve the cord.

After you have done this exercise a few times, your unconscious will automatically know which parts of your body to send energy to. So instead of moving consciously through your whole body, your basic intention to create a deep relaxed state will do the work for you. In a wave of psychic energy, relaxation will wash over all the parts of your body, and you will relax in a matter of moments.

One of my clients tried this exercise excitedly, and immediately fell asleep. In fact, every time he does it he still falls asleep. You have to understand that this guy is an insomniac. It just goes to show you, psychic energy knows what you need.

If you find yourself falling asleep, and you don't need sleep, try stepping up your active concentration as you go through the different parts of your body. This is a relaxing and focusing exercise. Yes, you are relaxing, but your mind is actively focused on molding and sending the energy to specific places while your body is focusing on deep breathing. This activity takes energy and inner concentration.

AT A GLANCE
Relaxing with Universal Energy

Step One Create your sacred space.

Step Two Lie down and get into a basic receptive state by listening to your breathing.

Step Three Create a ball of light four or five feet above your body. Create a cord connecting the ball of psychic energy to the top of your head, your heart, or your solar plexus.

Step Four Use the energy to surround yourself with a comfortable womb or protective cloud.

Step Five Concentrating on each part of your body, send the energy through the cord. Visualize it breaking up stress and releasing blocks in that particular area.

Step Six Stay relaxed for as long as you like. End your session by closing your sacred space.

Step Seven Write in your journal.

Psychic Workout

Grounding

In my many travels I have relaxed, meditated, and done readings in some very odd places: at the beach, in hotel rooms, on fire escapes, in airplanes. But my most expansive and transcending experience occurred while I was doing this exercise on a mountaintop in Los Angeles. Sitting on a rock, overlooking a canyon, surrounded by grass and trees, with the bright blue sky above me, I felt connected to everything, as though my consciousness expanded and became part of the trees, the birds, the sky, the canyon below. I literally felt ten feet tall!

You, too, can have this sort of transcending experience. After you have the steps down pat, you can do this exercise anywhere. It is designed to get psychic energy flowing through you, from the sky to the earth and back again, with you as the conduit. It involves deep breathing, which wakes up parts of you that are sleeping. This is great for developing all those different psychic abilities I mentioned in chapter 1—clairvoyance, clairaudience, clairsentience. When you're finished, you'll feel both energized and grounded, centered, and balanced within yourself.

If you read a lot of spiritual or meditation books, chances are that you have run into some variation of this workout. The idea of putting down roots has been around forever. My particular version is very stream-of-consciousness and unregimented.

After you create your sacred space and are in a deep state, start by standing up or sitting with your back straight. Close your eyes and take a few deep breaths. Then visually create a tube extending from the top of your head way up into the universe. Open the tube and fill yourself with pure psychic energy. Let it pour into your body.

As the energy reaches your feet, open up the other end of the tube and send it way down into the ground. Let all the energy drain from your tube into the ground.

Next, with the tube at your feet still open, pull warm, earthy energy back up from deep in the ground—like two miles down. Let it calm you as it makes its way through your body, exiting from the tube at the top of your head, way up into the universe.

Do this a few times, and when you understand the cycle, speed it up a bit and coordinate it with your breaths. Pull the energy in from the tube at the top of your head as you take a deep breath in. Expel the energy into the ground as you breathe out. Pull the energy up from your feet as you breathe in; release the energy at the top of your head as you breathe out.

When you have a comfortable flow going, stay there, or speed it up even more so that the pace is strong, comfortable, but slightly forced. After a few minutes, you'll feel very alive. If you're a bit lightheaded, it's probably OK, as long as you're not driving or operating any heavy machinery! After a few minutes, open both ends of your tube, slow your breathing down, and come back to the here and now.

When you are ready to end your session, pull the universal energy around you like a protective shield, and then write in your journal.

After you have done this once or twice, you will start to find a perfect pace that will create a solid flow in which you feel expanded and your inner senses are crisp and alive.

AT A GLANCE
Grounding

Step One Create your sacred space and get into a basic receptive state.

Step Two Standing or sitting straight, create a tube at the top of your head going way up into the universe. Pull psychic energy from the tube down through your body.

Step Three Open up the tube at the soles of your feet and let the energy drain deep into the earth.

Step Four Pull the energy back up from the earth through the tube at your feet, and send it through your body. Let it shoot out the tube at the top of your head, way into the universe.

Step Five When you understand the cycle, speed up the process and connect it with your breaths, pulling the energy in as you inhale, and expelling the energy as you exhale, alternating directions with each breath.

Step Six When you are ready to stop, to slow your breathing down, open both ends of the tube and return to normal.

Step Seven When you are ready to end your session, pull the universal energy around you to create a protective shield and . . .

Step Eight Write in your journal.

Psychic Workout
In and Up

Here's another way to cultivate your connection to psychic energy. Each person has a natural inborn way that works best for him or her, and this is just another method for you to try and see if it fits for you. You are going to focus your inner awareness into the sky and the stars. Try it and see if you feel your inner senses wake up as you project your consciousness way up into the universe.

This is a consciousness-expanding exercise, not an out-of-body experience. Your mind can go anywhere and not leave the couch. Don't expect anything far out, or you'll probably be disappointed.

Begin by creating your sacred space. Get into a basic meditative state by finding a comfortable rhythm to your deep breathing. It is important to keep this comfortable rhythm going throughout this workout. As you follow the steps and get into a deeper and deeper awareness, let this breathing become an unconscious routine.

Create a cylinder or tube going from the top of your head way up into the universe. With your eyes closed, send your consciousness up the tube about four feet. Take a moment to adjust to this height, using your inner awareness. Observe what your inner senses see, hear, and feel at this expanded level.

Now expand up the tube (past the ceiling) into the sky, just above the trees, houses, and buildings. Take a few moments to adjust your awareness. Using your inner senses, observe what you see, hear, and feel. Can you see the tops of the buildings, feel the wind, hear the birds?

As you continue to breathe deeply, let your consciousness shoot up to the clouds. Spend a few moments checking it out up there. Let your inner senses do the work as you collect your impressions.

The last step up your travel tube is up to the stars. Feel your consciousness expand way out into unlimited space. Note what you see, hear, and feel with your inner senses.

When you are ready to end your session, shrink your consciousness back into your body and visualize a protective shield of universal energy around you. Close your sacred space and write in your journal.

AT A GLANCE
In and Up!

Step One Begin by creating your sacred space. Get into a basic meditative state by finding a comfortable rhythm to your deep breathing.

Step Two Create a cylinder or tube going from the top of your head way up into the universe.

Step Three With your eyes closed, send your consciousness up the tube about four feet. Observe what your inner senses see, hear, and feel at this expanded level.

Step Four Now expand up the tube (past the ceiling) into the sky. Using your inner senses, observe what you see, hear, and feel.

Step Five Let your consciousness shoot up to the clouds; collect your inner impressions.

Step Six Expand up your travel tube way out into unlimited space. Note what you see, hear, and feel with your inner senses.

Step Seven When you are ready to end your session, shrink your consciousness back into your body and visualize a protective shield of universal energy around you.

Step Eight Close your sacred space and write in your journal.

Psychic Workout
Inner Listening

We are so used to seeing with our eyes and hearing with our ears that we rarely awaken our inner perceptions. But as you learned in chapter 1, we were born with these inner senses wired into our brain. This exercise is just going to awaken the ability that is already in there.

As you do this exercise, you'll see how simple it is to see, feel, and hear things from inside your body. Inner Listening is designed to awaken your inner sight (clairvoyance), your inner hearing (clairaudience), and your inner knowing (clairsentience). Most of the time, these senses are working unconsciously. This exercise lets us access these senses to make conscious observations.

You can do this exercise lying down, sitting comfortably, or standing up. Experiment by moving to different rooms and changing your position. In fact, the best way to do this exercise is to do it in unfamiliar places like hotel rooms, friends' apartments, your family's yard. That way you'll always be observing new things and you will never be on automatic pilot. The more you experiment, the more you'll learn.

Begin by creating your sacred space and getting into a basic receptive state. With your eyes closed throughout this exercise, focus on your breathing. Feel it as the force of life. Feel this from inside your body and inside your head. Feel your belly rise and fall; feel your lungs expand and contract.

When you are comfortable, bring your attention to the outside of your body. Slowly explore your body's entire surface. Feel the pressure of your body on the couch; feel your clothing on your legs; feel the air on your face and the light on your closed eyes. Note your perceptions.

When you are finished, shift your awareness to the environment just outside your body. Observe the space directly behind your body, in front of your body, on each side of you, above, and underneath. As you see, feel, and hear the different areas around your body, what are your impressions? Are certain areas expansive? Light? Thick?

I do this part by getting into feeling as though I have a million tiny eyes all over my skin. When I want to observe a particular area around me, I open the little eyes that correspond with that part of my skin. After you do this workout a couple of times, you'll know what works best for you.

Now for the fun part. When you are ready, extend your awareness to the whole room around you. Feel the walls, the windows, the doors, the ceiling. As you slowly examine the room with your inner senses, what do you observe? Do you see the walls? Does a doorway feel different from a window? When your inner senses are developed, you can feel the difference between the two. You don't have to be some psychic genius, you just have to be in possession of some concentration and courage.

For the first few times you do this, end here. Then, once you are adept at it and your inner awareness is active and itching to get out of the house, take it for a walk. Expand into the hallway and out the window, through the ceiling and the floor. What do you see? What do you feel? What do you hear beyond the four walls? Don't worry about being right or wrong, and don't expect to always observe concrete things. Much of your perception will be subtle.

AT A GLANCE
Inner Listening

Step One Create your sacred space and get into a basic receptive state.

Step Two With your eyes closed, focus on your breathing. With your inner senses, observe each breath and the rise and fall of your belly.

Step Three Bring your attention to the outside of your body. Observe each part of your body as it comes in contact with the environment.

Step Four Bring your awareness to the environment just outside your body. Explore the space behind you, in front of you, around you, and above you.

Step Five Expand your awareness to the whole room. Using your inner senses, see, feel, and hear the walls, doors, and windows.

Step Six End here, or expand into the hallway and out the window, through the ceiling and the floor. What are you receiving, beyond what your five senses could normally pick up?

Step Seven End your session by shrinking your awareness back into your body and using it to create a shield of protection around yourself.

Step Eight Write in your journal.

You've just finished the basics. You accomplished a lot! Don't feel that just because they are basic that they are less important. From the minute you started this chapter, you took charge of your psychic destiny.

My friend Jennifer has been working with these exercises for more than two years. She went through each and every exercise that you are going to do, and ended up picking these early ones as her favorite and most effective. Why? Because she is so naturally grounded and focused that these less complex, less structured exercises really let her get outside herself and let go. She would do the more advanced workouts with longer steps and try to get them so perfect that she forgot why she was doing them in the first place. This is your book, and this is your psychic ability—follow your heart, you know best.

You are now psychically savvy—you know how to create a great psychic foundation and turn the energy on and off, so you're probably eager to start using it in your life. You want to know how to pick up your next job opportunity, find your next girlfriend or boyfriend, or talk to your spirit guides and angels—which we'll get to in chapter 4. There's just one more thing to learn first, though, and that's crossing the valley of disbelief and clearing out your psychic receptors so that you will receive clear information. No matter how gung ho we are to develop our psychicness, we all carry around fears and beliefs that can hamper this growth—that is why it is even more important for skeptics to create a neutral place before doing their psychic workouts, as we did earlier in this chapter.

The next chapter will help you work through different beliefs and fears you may be holding that could get in the way of developing your abilities as far as you'd like. You will also do some exercises designed to help you figure out what is truly important to you. It's a little like learning about your personal operating system and decoding your inner spiritual handbook. The techniques in chapter 3 will balance out your psychic potential with inner strength and knowhow. Then you will be psychically unstoppable!

Troubleshooting

You may have had a very cool first experience where you saw, heard, or felt something with your inner senses—or you may not have felt anything. That doesn't mean you didn't make the connection, it just means that you may need a few more sessions before your inner senses tune in to the energy. Before you get too disappointed that bells didn't go off in your head, try again. The more comfortable you become with the process itself, the easier it will be to pick up information.

I have one client who had such a hard time giving up control that she spent two whole weeks learning to sit still and allowing the universe to flow through her without trying to control the flow. She needed to learn how to manipulate the energy as it moved through her without cutting it off. She started off slowly, doing minute-long sessions. All these false ideas of what was supposed to happen were getting in her way. Once she let go of her expectations, her sessions lengthened and began to be effective. If you're having a hard time sitting through these exercises for any reason, do them for one or two minutes at a time. One minute is better than none, and besides, you'll get better after a few sessions and then you can lengthen your session time.

It will also be helpful to remember that *perception is everything*. Many beginners see the abilities of professional psychics as unattainable. If you think it is difficult to connect with psychic energy, then it will be. If you think you aren't good enough to access it, then you won't be. If you believe in yourself and your natural ability, then it will not even be an issue. Need I say more?

chapter three

the other side is right around the corner

___

Early in my psychic career, I was struggling a lot financially. I was running around at breakneck speeds trying to coordinate a lot of small jobs and making little money. I felt like I was chasing my tail, and there was no end in sight. I was starting out as a tarot card reader and doing some writing, acting, and standup comedy on the side. To top it off, in order to make ends meet I took a part-time job showing expensive real estate.

Tired, frustrated, and broke, I went to a wonderful psychic, Corinne Jeffrey, and asked her, "Why is it that I am so good at so many things and I still struggle all the time?" Her response was this: "Because you believe that you have to struggle to make a living, and in order to be successful at what you love, you're trying to keep pace with the rest of the world."

Aha! It was as if she had gone fishing in my head and pulled out a live one. Before she said that, I had no conscious idea that I even had that belief. In that instant, it dawned on me. "I don't have to struggle, it will all just come to me!"

Our beliefs create our reality: Within a week, I was booked for a high-paying tarot event; within two weeks I had steady employment reading cards at a hot Manhattan nightclub; within four months I was offered a steady acting gig and quit my real estate job. I've been a full-time psychic ever since.

God only knows how much struggle I would've continued to create for myself had I not asked that simple question—and that is why this chapter is so necessary. You can do all the psychic workouts you want, but if there is an unconscious negative or limiting belief floating around in your head that is going to negate the work, all you are going to get for your efforts is frustration.

We all recognize certain negative beliefs and fears that we live with every day. But the most damaging fears lie in our unconscious. A fear of hospitals or a fear of heights, for instance, are beliefs that people live with every day. We are usually fully aware of these limitations. Unconscious beliefs, on the other hand, are deep thoughts we have about reality that we may not even recognize we hold. I have a friend who believes that hard work is never recognized; a client who believes she must act as a different person outside than she is inside in order to survive in this world. These core beliefs make up our internal belief systems. This chapter is about accessing those beliefs, seeing them for what they truly are, and then getting past whichever ones we must overcome in order to set free our psychic selves.

Negative or limiting beliefs stem from three sources. The first is parental programming. The family in which we were each brought up possessed its own unique outlook on how the world works. According to this outlook, as children we learned that certain things are right and wrong; that reality is based on a specific defined set of rules. At a young age, we accepted these rules without question. If you grew up with a father who worked hard for a living, you may have learned that making a living is difficult. If you were brought up in a traditional household, you may have learned that men and women have a defined set of responsibilities. If you had older brothers and sisters who bullied you, you may now still feel like the world victimizes people. As adults, these rules or beliefs from our childhoods are so deeply ingrained in our heads that we can't see them for what they really are—thoughts about reality.

The second source of limiting beliefs are those impressions that were useful when we first picked them up but have since outgrown. For example, as children we all learned that we cannot cross the street without an adult. At one time that was a good belief for us to have, but holding on to beliefs longer than we need to stops us from growing. Some of the more ambiguous childhood beliefs are more difficult to notice: Beliefs like "I struggle to learn" translate into "I've struggled with learning, as long as I can remember." You may have had a hard time reading and writing in first grade, and that is where the belief originated, but that belief, left unchecked, will poison your experience for years before you finally recognize it.

Finally, we accumulate limiting beliefs by not consciously examining our lives and what makes us tick. As adults, we experience new things every day. We go to work, meet new people, get married, have children. The way we handle ourselves during these events is based on our thoughts and beliefs. You may never have had a fear of intimacy until you broke up with your first love; you may never have had a fear of failure until you failed the entrance exam to that special program you so desperately wanted to get into. You can pick up limiting beliefs with every experience. Every day we learn new things, although usually they aren't as traumatic as these examples. If we don't examine these responses, fears, and beliefs as we experience them, we may carry those new thoughts with us throughout our lives. They will continue to shape our experiences in negative ways until we recognize them and eliminate them.

Unconscious beliefs remain just that unless we go searching for them. This search can only work if we make a conscious effort to see our thought patterns as they run deep, beyond our everyday reality. They can be seen with a few simple exercises—and believe me, they are simple. But if you don't do this, you may be walking around thinking thoughts that literally become obstacles to your own success as a human being. By getting to know what your negative thought habits are, you can work to eliminate them. As you understand where these thoughts come from, you can change them. You can rewrite what you think, and create a more successful foundation for your life.

No, I'm not just trying to make you a better person! There *is* a psychic payoff in all this. Psychically, you are a conduit, a magnet, a channel for psychic information and universal energy. But if you're unaware of your deep patterns, you have a lot of stuff clogging your psychic channel. First, you will not be able to attract a lot of psychic information if you are unable to get control of your patterns—that in itself is frustrating and can be mistaken for a lack of psychic ability. Everyone has psychic ability; the problem is that you may not be clear enough to receive energy. Second, if you are blocked by limiting beliefs, you will not be able to read the psychic information you do receive in a clear and balanced way. You may think you're seeing it all, when in fact you're just picking up your own stuff and chasing your own tail.

There is no magic at work here. Simply recognizing your limiting thoughts and getting these deep-seated negative beliefs out of your unconscious will bring clarity to your life. As you let these beliefs go, your life will flow with psychic energy and success; things will come to you more easily; and you'll be able to perceive things more clearly. Negative events will begin to melt away, and all your daily experiences will be more positive and life-affirming. And once your channel is clear, you can work on getting even more psychic.

The first two exercises in this chapter will show you how to recognize your unconscious thought patterns and belief systems. That way, you can get them out in the open where you can work with them constructively. By figuring out what your negative patterns are and where

The Ten Best Questions to Ask the Universe

One Is the moon really made of green cheese? If so, is it imported?

Two Is there really a man in the moon? If so, does he need crackers?

Three When You invented the Bee Gees, what were You thinking?

Four Do You like the *I Love Lucy* episodes we sent You?

Five Is Stonehenge Your idea of a wristwatch?

Six Are all the planets just one big unfinished game of billiards?

Seven How old is Dick Clark?

Eight If someone sneezed in space, and nobody heard it, would it make a sound?

Nine Who coined the expression "The devil made me do it"?

Ten If a plane leaves Dallas at 2:45 P.M. traveling north, and a spaceship leaves Alpha Centauri at 3:00, will the two aircraft intersect by dinnertime, or is everyone on board going to get really hungry?

they come from, you can review them and find a new perspective. You'll ditch the bad stuff, and you'll begin to replace it with a more positive foundation.

Next you'll move into goal-setting—three exercises to help you discover who you truly are. Finally, you'll learn to make affirmations and visualizations that will become the catalyst for much of this change. They are your inner tools for building a fulfilled You.

The first time you do these exercises will be an interesting experience—to say the least. First, you'll get into your regular basic receptive state as you do with all the other psychic workouts. Then you'll ask yourself a series of questions. In a stream-of-consciousness form, you'll write down the answers. You will be connecting to your Higher Self to get true and powerful information about your internal operating system. Your Higher Self is the You that created you; it is the part of you that is with God. It is unlimited and whole. It holds all the answers to who you are and what your destiny is.

In addition to clearing out a lot of gunk gumming your internal carburetor, these exercises will be helpful to you any time you go through a transition in your life and need a shot of clarity. When you are desperately seeking a new job; when you feel low in energy and are thinking about making a change to jump start yourself; when you are about to get married, graduate from school, have a child—all these new situations will bring up new learning experiences and new fears and beliefs. Don't go through them unaware. By doing these exercises before or after a transition, you ensure that any emerging thoughts or fears about the transition are recognized and worked on. Think about how easy a transition to a new job would be if you understood beforehand all the fears, limiting beliefs, and negative thoughts you had about making the change.

Discovering Unconscious Thought Patterns

The first time I did this exercise was way into my psychic career, so it goes to show you that no matter how developed you are, you still keep learning. I got into a deep state and asked myself what my beliefs were about my success and happiness, just because I wanted to know what was floating around in my head. What came out really surprised me. What I believed at the time was: "There is really no good reason for me to be happy, happiness doesn't come to everybody. No one can really have it all." When I asked myself the origins of that belief, I discovered that this picture was what I saw all around me when I was a very little girl. Grown-up people were content but not happy. They were always making compromises as far as their happiness and freedom. When we are younger, we are more perceptive than we realize!

One of my busier-than-busy clients did the same exercise and realized that he had the longstanding belief: "I never have enough time to do anything." He has since changed that to: "I have more than enough time. I just need to manage my time and enjoy the time I have during the day." Since he started working with these exercises, he is much more peaceful and has more hope and faith in life.

Psychic Workout

Fears and Beliefs

This exercise will put you in touch with your limiting beliefs and negative thought patterns. First, write the following questions in your journal, leaving space for the answers. Don't look at the page filled with blank spaces and go nuts. There's no need to address them all in one session.

1. *What are my beliefs about my love life?*
2. *What are my beliefs about my career?*
3. *What are my beliefs about myself?*
4. *What are my fears about my love life?*
5. *What are my fears about my career?*
6. *What are my fears about myself?*

If you'd like, you can list additional questions concerning certain issues or problems you are having: your relationship with your boyfriend or girlfriend, your weight, a special work project, whatever. This exercise works like a charm for anything and everything.

To begin, create your sacred space and get into a basic receptive state. Concentrate on the first question on your list. With your eyes closed, repeat the question in your head a few times. Record everything you feel, both your negative and positive feelings. Don't judge yourself, edit your words, or think too much. If you are hesitant and nothing comes into your head, you are letting your brain get in the way. Don't despair! The first question is the toughest. Just begin writing, and the block should go away. When you have written everything that comes to mind, go to the next question and repeat the process.

When you have done this for all your questions, reread each of your answers. Leave the positive beliefs alone, but for each negative belief, go back and ask yourself the big one: Where did that belief originate? Get into a deep state and let the truth flow. Was it when you were six and your mother yelled at you? Was it when you failed your first chemistry exam? Was it when you broke up with your first boyfriend/girlfriend? In your deep state, the origins of these beliefs should be as apparent as the beliefs themselves. Write everything down.

Once you have your negative beliefs and their origins on paper, look at them for what they truly are. This will take some quality thinking. Since you now know what caused you to take on these beliefs in the first place, you can separate the original experience from the belief you carry with you and create a new belief that will better suit your success. To do that, take a moment to figure out what you would like to believe about your love life, your career, or yourself. Write these beliefs down.

Put your new list of beliefs everywhere—on your refrigerator door, your phone, and your bathroom mirror. Begin applying these new beliefs in your life, one experience at a time, until you are doing it as second nature. This may take some getting used to, but with enough reminders lying around it becomes a lot easier.

AT A GLANCE
Fears and Beliefs

Step One Write down fundamental questions in your notebook.

Step Two Create your sacred space and get into a basic receptive state.

Step Three With your eyes closed, repeat each question in your head a few times. Write down everything you feel.

Step Four Reread each of your answers. In your deep state, ask yourself, "Where did this belief originate?"

Step Five Quality thinking time. Look at the beliefs and their origins for what they truly are. Figure out what you *want* to believe, and write it down.

Step Six End your session by recording in your journal how you feel about these major revelations. Rewrite your new list of beliefs and place them in visible spots in your environment. Look at them often.

You've just examined your core belief system. Now you're ready to examine it in relation to very specific events or occurrences in your life. What you'll be doing here is sort of a reality check. You are going to go through all the things in your life that you are not 100 percent thrilled with and ask yourself what your thoughts are on those subjects. In doing so, you'll discover why you have attracted these things into your life in the first place. Once you understand your unconscious motivations, you can easily change them . . . and then you will begin to see all sorts of new things in your life that you like better! When you recognize bad beliefs and start to get rid of them, you'll be able to replace them with beliefs that will bring you more success.

Psychic Workout

What's Not Working in Your Life

Ready to put your finger on all the things in your life you're not happy with, and then get rid of them? To begin, make a list in your journal of everything in your life that you dislike in any way. What makes you feel uncomfortable? Unhappy? Dissatisfied? Afraid? Leave a space on the page after each item. Here are some examples:

My old car
That extra ten pounds
My job
My income

Now create your sacred space and get into a basic receptive state. With your eyes closed, concentrate on your first topic and think, "What exactly am I unhappy about?" Repeat the question in your head a few times as you breathe deeply. The answer should pop into your head. Write it down: I hate that my car always breaks down and that it is an ugly color. *When you finish one topic, go on to all the others.*

Examine your completed list; then go back to the first topic and ask, "What are the beliefs I have that caused this feeling to occur?" Repeat the question a few times as you breathe deeply. Let the answer pop into your head naturally, and write it down. If it doesn't, try the question: "Why is this in my life?" You may get something like this: The reason I have a broken-down ugly car is because I believe I am never going to be able to afford a new one and so I have to hold on to this one as long as it works. *Wow, that's a powerful belief keeping you chained to that car!*

Once you've explored your negative beliefs about parts of your life you dislike, you're ready to write a corresponding list of positive beliefs that will lay a strong foundation for successful living. For each item you feel negatively about, envision a positive truth about it—anything you can easily start to believe, even if you do not believe it now. My car gets me where I want to go. Even though it's old, it works great! I know I will get a brand-new car and be like that woman in the Saturn commercial.

Write down these new beliefs on a separate sheet of paper. Make sure they have no limiting language. No negatives such as "I do not . . ." or "Never again . . ." And make sure they're not written in a perpetually future tense. No "One day . . ." or "In two weeks . . ." If you say something will happen in two weeks, then the belief will always be two weeks into the future and never come to be in the here and now. If you feel you need time to get used to these positive statements, give a time limit, like "Within two years . . . (and make sure you count down the days)" or "By 2001 . . ." By doing it this way, the time will eventually come upon you in the present.

Study these new beliefs side by side with your old ones. Look at what's been inside your head! Now take the old beliefs and rip them up. Burn them and bury the ashes. Throw them out the window (then pick up the litter and dispose of it properly, of course).

Now the only thing you have left is your list of new beliefs. Study it a million times. (OK, I'm exaggerating, but repetition is important.) You must completely let go of the old beliefs and live by the new ones. As you let go of the old beliefs, you'll let go of the corresponding things you don't like, and you'll find yourself surrounded by things you really do enjoy. In addition to resolving nagging feelings of unhappiness about your car, you'll feel clearer and more focused on what is truly You.

One of my clients, Joanna, spent the summer in Europe visiting her family and doing this exercise over and over. Whenever she had a negative belief or thought, she wrote it down and burned it. She was constantly walking around with an ash tray, and her cousins thought she was nuts. But at the end of the summer, not only did she have a completely different attitude, she had figured out what she wanted to do in life and came home excited to begin earning a teaching degree.

AT A GLANCE
What's Not Working in Your Life

Step One Write a list of everything in your life that you dislike in any way.

Step Two Create your sacred space and get into a basic receptive state.

Step Three With your eyes closed, concentrate on each topic and think, "What exactly am I unhappy about?" Repeat the question in your head a few times as you breathe deeply. Record your answers.

Step Four For each topic, ask, "What are the beliefs I have that caused this to occur?" Repeat the question a few times as you breathe deeply and record your answers.

Step Five Write a corresponding list of positive beliefs.

Step Six Spend a few minutes studying the new beliefs—they are yours!

Step Seven End your session with a writing jaunt in your journal. Burn or throw away your old beliefs. Study your new beliefs throughout the day.

I know that delving into your unconscious can be difficult, so pat yourself on the back; you are doing great work. Besides, you're finished with that part! You now know what you believe, and you can go on to work with what is important to you. I know goal-setting doesn't sound like a psychic exercise, but there is a very good reason for it to be here. You can be overflowing with positive beliefs and have all the psychic ability in the world, but if you don't know where to focus that ability, it will not help you get what you want. If you have a concise and focused goal, your psychic senses will constantly be working to fulfill that goal, whether you know it or not.

Discovering Your Path: Destiny and Goal-setting

If you're like most people, you probably already have an idea of what your destiny is; you just don't realize it. Your destiny is apparent in your current dreams, goals, special skills, and talents. But people often don't recognize the link between something being important to them and that thing actually pointing out their life's path. Your destiny is due north on your internal compass. You are programmed for your destiny—if the universe wants you to be an accountant, it gives you a love of numbers, not a great voice. The singers get the voice, the accountants get the numbers. There is only one exception to this, and that is the singing accountants!

If you don't know what direction you are headed in, or if you're not comfortable with the path you seem to be on, you can feel lost, stagnant, and confused. All this diffused energy can adversely affect your psychic senses. Your destiny is such a part of you that denying it can cause many problems. A healthy understanding of your path will enable you to follow your intuition with a sense of peace and expansion.

I can't tell you how many clients I have who work for big corporations but are chomping at the bit to write for a living or pining to start a business with their spouse. These are good ideas. So why are these people still unhappily working for someone else? Because they don't realize they are ignoring their destiny! They will be happier, have more free time, and still make a good living if they begin that writing career or start up that company.

Many of my clients come to me on the verge of big transitions in their lives. They are ready for change, yet they have no idea how to create it. One of my clients said that the reason she comes to me is not because I'm usually right, but because I remind her of who she is. She is struggling with her creativity, is somewhat afraid to take risks, has a full-time job to pay the bills, and cannot see when the struggle will end. I help her separate the unnecessary junk from her higher path.

Psychic ability is very inspiring when it is working in conjunction with destiny. You do not have to struggle your way through life. You can use your psychic ability to manifest your goals and achieve your destiny—no matter how impossible it may seem. Using universal energy enables you to bypass the logical rules many of us live by, letting you learn and grow, accomplish the most seemingly impossible tasks with ease and grace, and fulfill your purpose.

To receive your destiny, you have to be comfortable with it, and with living up to your potential. Some people have a more natural connection to that potential than others do. To me, potential and destiny are one and the same. Fully living who you are means focusing on the right path and doing it all the way. Some people live to their potential and others don't. Some people are afraid of their potential.

These exercises are going to fix all that. You are going to experience the full and complete You. You're going to become comfortable with that You by experiencing how you will think and feel being the You you are meant to be. As you get to know this state of oneness, you will

Miracle Boxes

Want to make miracles happen, fast? Get two small boxes, bowls, or baskets—one for wishes, one for goals. Create your sacred space, close your eyes, take a few deep breaths, and awaken your inner senses. Then—with all your conscious intention—write out your wishes and goals on tiny pieces of paper. As you drop each piece into the box, imagine energizing it with pure psychic energy. See how quickly these wishes come to pass. Do the same with the things in your life you appreciate. The more you appreciate things, the more things will come to you!

automatically start reflecting that into your everyday experience and seeing your reality transcend into this wonderful potential.

Writing a list of concrete goals will help you achieve that You. Writing goals is simple, but making sure they are *your* goals may not be so easy. You have to make sure they are what you want rather than social or parental programming. You do that by actually experiencing the perfect You in the exercise called Becoming Comfortable with Your Destiny. Take your time with this section and enjoy getting to know your Self.

After you have written your goals, you will see your path clearing in front of you. Reevaluate your goal lists every few months, and do these exercises every time you achieve a short-term or long-term goal. That way, you will forever be creating your future in a fluid motion. As you progress, using your goals as steps, you will find it easier to get where you want to be. You'll get further than you ever dreamed!

Psychic Workout

Writing Your Inspiration Crest

The first step of goal-setting is to set up the qualities you want to see in your life. An inspiration crest is a one-paragraph statement that serves as a reminder of what you feel to be truly important in your life. This statement is your opportunity to express what is important to you—to express what is important to your soul. It's a motto that is a reflection of your Higher Self and of your highest ideals. As you live by this motto, you'll begin to notice that all the events and experiences in your life will synthesize with it.

This statement does two things. One, it reveals any events in your life that don't correspond to it—which will enable you to get rid of any experiences that don't fit in. Two, it serves as a message to your psychic self to attract only the events that are in harmony with it.

To begin, write the heading "My Inspiration Crest" in your journal. Then write three questions on the page, leaving space for the answers.

What do I want out of my life?
What virtues are important to me?
What inspires and moves me?

Create your sacred space and get into a deep meditative state. When you are ready, bring your attention to the first question. Repeat it in your head a few times. Let the answer fill your head. Write down what you see and feel. This is what my question-and-answer session looks like:

- *What do I want out of my life?*
  I want to have the freedom to write and create with success. I want to be able to live and be and do what is important to me without restriction. I want to be able to fulfill my destiny.
- *What virtues are important to me?*
  Truth, honesty, integrity.
- *What inspires and moves me?*
  A deep connection to the universe (my spirit guides, God). Helping, inspiring, and healing others. Helping the world reflect truth and love.

After you have explored all three questions, shape your answers into a paragraph reflecting your needs. Take it slow and careful. You will be looking at this statement a lot! My paragraph looks like this:

It is important for me to have the freedom to shape how and where I want to live, and to use my strengths to teach and heal others. It is important that integrity and truth are guideposts in my daily existence, not only for me but also for those I work with and play with. I need to have a deep understanding of my experiences and those of the people around me in order to operate on a deeper inspired level.

My inspiration crest sounds wonderful, and so will yours. Write it out and put it all over the place—on your microwave, your StairMaster, the dashboard of your car. Reread it every day to remind yourself how special you are.

It is important that you remember this is your Highest ideal. Every day you read it, every day you aspire to it, you will see your life begin to flow and harmonize with the words.

AT A GLANCE
Writing Your Inspiration Crest

Step One In your journal, write the heading "My Inspiration Crest" and the three questions listed above.

Step Two Create your sacred space and get into a basic receptive state.

Step Three Repeat each question in your head a few times, and record your answers.

Step Four Shape these answers into a paragraph. This is your motto.

Step Five End your session with a quick jaunt in your journal.

Many of us are wary of following our hearts—we fear failure, rejection, isolation, and all sorts of other things. We may have taken on a lot of social programming that is very different from our true selves. If this sounds like you, then you may do these exercises and neither trust nor believe what you see. This next exercise is crucial, because it helps you not only discover who you are but live it. The first time you do this workout you will experience your destiny. Do it over and over again until you are comfortable with all that you are.

Psychic Workout
Becoming Comfortable with Your Destiny

Begin by creating your sacred space and getting into a basic receptive state. Sit comfortably with your eyes closed. Visualize a pod or a cloud in front of you. It is big enough for your body to fit comfortably inside. It is made of pure universal energy. This pod is your perfect world.

Now imagine putting a perfect You inside the pod. Take a few moments to explore the perfect You, putting together a fabulous picture. What would the perfect You do? How would the perfect You act? What would the perfect You look like? What would the perfect You feel like when doing what the perfect You is doing? Talk this description into a tape recorder, or write it down or draw it in your notebook. Be really specific. Here's mine:

> I have already published a few successful books. I see myself lecturing a large group of people. I am having loads of fun, and the audience is learning a lot. I also see myself on the set of a TV show. I am rehearsing something. I am laughing with the other people on the set. I feel successful, beautiful, and empowered—like I can do anything.
>
> I have a steady beau. He is thirty-seven years old, five-foot-ten, with a build on the thin side and dark curly hair. He wears ripped jeans, and he is very creative and successful and very caring. I sing opera as a hobby and play the piano skillfully; I work out often and feel great about my body.

I can go on and on, and so should you. Really get into it! Truly feel what it is like having your perfect life—no matter how different it is from the one you live now. What you picture in your perfect world is the You that you deserve, nothing less.

You might read my description and think it is egomaniacal to want to be so good at so many things or be so perfect and be proud of it. I've got news for you—there is no reason not to want the world and be good at everything. That just makes a successful person. You know you will never achieve anything that you are uncomfortable with, so get used to being great, and great things will come to you. If you feel uneasy about this, just don't share your imagined future with anyone.

After you have created the perfect You in the perfect world, pull your imaginary pod around you and feel what it is like to exist in that dimension. Own it completely. Do this for a few minutes. It will have a cumulative effect: A few minutes a day of this perfection will translate into concrete changes in your life.

When you are finished, leave the pod around you so that you can be perfect all day long. End your session by writing in your journal. This journal entry is important, because you have just discovered exactly what you want to see in your life. Even though it may be very different from the life you have now, write it all down anyway. You'll use your psychic ability to achieve this perfect You in the second half of this book.

AT A GLANCE

Becoming Comfortable with Your Destiny

Step One Create a sacred space and get into a basic meditative state.

Step Two With your eyes closed, visualize a pod or cloud with a perfect You inside.

Step Three Imagine the perfect You, in close detail.

Step Four Pull the pod around you and feel what it is like in this perfect world. Do this for a few minutes.

Step Five When you are finished, leave the pod around you and end your session by writing in your journal.

So you've cleared your channel, and you have a sense of your destiny. You have a personal motto to live by, and you've seen a glimpse of the perfect You. Now here's where we get extremely practical and write out a list of goals or steps that will get you to that perfect place. Having concrete steps and goals is important for two reasons. One, as you ground yourself with solid goals, you will naturally take actions that fulfill these goals and bring you loads of happiness. And two, setting goals is like telling your unconscious, psychic senses to be on the lookout for these opportunities.

Psychic Workout
Setting Goals

To begin, create your sacred space and get into a deep receptive state. Take a few moments to connect with your Higher Self and your Higher Ideals by taking a deep breath and returning to the feeling you had when you did the Becoming Comfortable with Your Destiny exercise. Get in touch with who you are and what you want to see in your life now and in the future as you did with Becoming Comfortable with Your Destiny.

In your journal, write down a list of long-term goals that you want to accomplish in your future. Five years down the road is a good projection. That way, you don't risk creating goals that are way out of touch with your reality. Mine look like this:

A successful television show on the air.
Two or three successful books published.
A committed relationship with my soulmate.
At least one of the two children I am going to have.

Whatever you want is exactly what is perfect for you. You may want to have an MBA, you may want to have a successful teaching or law practice, you may want to get an education. You may want to buy a farm in Wyoming and work on letting go of some of the clutter in your life. Your goals don't have to make sense to anyone but you.

Next, put your long-term goals aside and make a list of short-term goals, specific steps it will take to achieve your long-term goals. Mine look like this:

Pitch my script ideas.
Get a good entertainment agent.
Write the best manuscript for this book; do everything I can to get this book in the hands of readers.

Work with universal energy every day and make sure I am clear and ready and open for a relationship.

When you have written all your goals, spend a minute or two energizing each one. To do this, imagine sending pure universal energy to each goal you have written on the page. End your session by surrounding yourself, visually, with a protective shield of universal energy. Close your sacred space and write in your journal.

AT A GLANCE
Setting Goals

Step One Create your sacred space and achieve a deep receptive state.

Step Two Take a few moments to connect with your Higher Self and your Higher ideals.

Step Three Write a list of long-term goals.

Step Four Write a list of short-term goals.

Step Five Energize your list of goals.

Step Six Visually surround yourself with a protective energy layer, close your sacred space, and write in your journal.

Keep your list of goals taped up around your house, on your mirrors, or on the ceiling above your bed. Be proud of yourself for all your efforts to accomplish these goals. Know that your psychic self began working with you to accomplish them the minute you wrote them on paper.

Affirmations and Visualizations:
The Little Engines That Could

Now you're clear to move on and fully explore your psychic side. To make doubly sure that you transition into your true Self with ease and grace, there is one more series of exercises you should learn—affirmations and visualizations. Affirmations and visualizations add elbow grease to all of the work you've been doing so far in this chapter. They are psychic power tools that will help you energize and achieve your goals, as well as clear away any leftover negative debris that may still be clogging your psychic channel.

You've eliminated much of this debris during the two workouts you did earlier on discovering your fears and beliefs. But sometimes clutter doesn't go away that easily. As you follow this chapter, it will become apparent which limiting beliefs and thought habits need a little extra prodding. You may feel resistance to letting go of some deeply ingrained fears or find it uncomfortable to believe some of your new positive beliefs. Affirmations and visualizations will help you. They are perfect tools to bring in on the spur of the moment.

An affirmation is a positive statement that becomes reality by being written and spoken over and over again with the full focus and intention of your psychic energy. A visualization is a mental image of a desired goal, which becomes reality when you picture or draw it with the full intention and power of your psychic energy. Affirmations and visualizations work on the principle that belief creates reality. You can use the power of your mind in connection with psychic energy to create whatever you want.

You may feel more comfortable with affirmations if you are a clairaudient or clairsentient person. If you are a clairvoyant or visual person, you may be more attracted to visualizations. One is not better than the other; most people work with both and find that variety is most effective in achieving success with affirmations and visualizations.

To work with affirmations and visualizations, you have to first know what you want, what is standing in the way of getting it, and how far you'll allow yourself to go, comfortably, to get those things. In other words, you have to have an understanding of your goals and your limitations—and work within your comfort zone. Once you begin to work with affirmations and visualizations, you'll feel the difference right away. Within a few weeks you'll begin to live more freely. Your fears and limiting beliefs will wash away; your goals will begin to come to fruition.

A word of caution. When you are working with affirmations and visualizations to reach a goal, overkill isn't healthy. You can put in all the effort you want—for a month or two, or if the goal is huge, even three months—but at some point you have to release the goal, phrase, or picture you are working with, even if it hasn't yet come to you. By ceasing to work with it and giving it to a higher source, you are effectively saying to the universe: *I've done my part, now do yours.* You are leaving space for psychic energy to do its job.

Visualize yourself handing the goal, phrase, or image to your angels or spirit guides. Imagine it floating away up into the clouds—or you can recite a statement directly to the universe. "OK, Spirit, I've done my work. I've cleared away the negatives, and I've given my full, concentrated effort to this goal, phrase, or image. I feel that I have done enough, and I feel good about it. I now release this goal to you. Thank you for bringing it to me. I'll occupy my time while you work on it, and when it gets here, I won't miss it."

Since you are awakening to your true psychic self, chances are you will be learning and growing at a fast pace, releasing old fears and beliefs and achieving your goals. For these affirmations and visualizations to work best, you should keep updating them, cutting out the ones that you no longer need, and adding new ones to reflect the new you. I do this two to four times a year—or whenever I am on the verge of a transition. This keeps your psychic flow open and working toward creating successful living.

Psychic Workout
Constructing Affirmations and Visualizations

It is up to you to create affirmations and visualizations that fit as perfectly in your mind as a good tool would in your hand. Affirmations and visualizations are only effective if you feel an internal connection to them and they are within your comfort zone. Those that really work are the ones that connect to the deepest part of who you are. The more they talk to you, and the more you feel them, the faster they come about.

FIRST, THE AFFIRMATIONS . . .

To create your best and most effective affirmations, take out your list of fears and beliefs from the Fears and Beliefs workout and your list of goals from the Long-Term and Short-Term Goals workout. Create your sacred space and get into a meditative state. Concentrate on each fear, limiting belief, and goal one at a time. For each item, ask yourself two questions:

- *What positive statement will free me to release this fear or belief or achieve this goal?*
- *What positive statement will empower me to release this fear or belief or achieve this goal?*

There is a subtle difference between a statement that will free you and one that will empower you. I may seem to be splitting hairs here, but in fact your brain may answer one of these questions more easily and concisely than the other. After you have done this exercise a few times, you'll know which one works better for you. Or you may use a combination of both.

When you get your answer, write it down. It is now your affirmation that corresponds to your specific fear, belief, or goal. For example, here's how I created an affirmation for success. My limiting belief on this issue, which I uncovered in the Fears and Beliefs exercise, was as follows:

> There is really no good reason for me to be happy; happiness doesn't come to everybody. No one can really have it all.

Here were my answers to the two questions:

- *I am free to be happy. I am free to accomplish everything I want.*
- *I can have it all.*

You may have to do a little rewriting of your answers in order to create perfect affirmations. An affirmation must be in the present tense with no negatives. I put those two answers together to create my success affirmation:

> I am free to be happy. I am free to accomplish everything I want. I can have it all. From now on I have it all.

Or:

> I am free, I have it all.

Notice that I have added, "From now on . . ." Statements like this reaffirm that from this day forth everything you want, you have. Even if it isn't so, you must phrase your statements as if they are happening in the here and now in order for them to happen in the here and now. These statements should also be positive: not "I don't see . . ." or "I have no . . ." Take your time and make sure you're comfortable with these statements and feel good about them.

Once you have created your affirmations, you can put them to work for you with any of the workouts that follow later in this chapter.

ON TO VISUALIZATIONS . . .

Visualizations involve creating a visual image of what you want to come into your life and then working with that image over and over to bring it into reality. Unlike affirmations, visualization work is done only with goals, not with fears and limiting beliefs. Goals are something you are trying to reach or change; fears and beliefs are thoughts you wish to release. Since thoughts are not visual images and you are not trying to bring them to you, I prefer not to create visual images of something you are working on getting rid of—it will just bring it to you even more. You're the boss, though, so feel free to create a visual image for anything you wish to create or become comfortable with.

Get the lists of goals you made when you did Setting Goals; create your sacred space and get into a deep state. Concentrate on these goals, one at a time. Repeat each goal in your head and let that specific goal create a mental picture in your head. Visualize it in great detail. Let a picture naturally develop. It is your visualization for that goal.

As with the affirmations, describe what you see in the present tense. As an example, we'll use my goal of having a successful TV show. After getting into a deep state, I closed my eyes and focused on that goal. The first time I did this, I immediately saw two images; I now use these images constantly to bring this goal to fruition.

The first image is of a meeting in a large office with three or four people besides me. My lawyer is next to me; the sun is streaming in through big windows; we are seated at a large, dark wooden desk. I am happily signing a contract; handshakes and smiles are flying around the room. The second image is of the set of the show I want to create. I see the couch, the windows, the kitchen. I am standing on the set; I am rehearsing the show.

The final step in the creation of a visualization is to put yourself in the picture. Pull the visual image around you and surround yourself with it, as you did in the Becoming Comfortable with Your Destiny workout, when you created the pod with the perfect You in it. Now you are living your visualization—in the here and now, you are living that goal. Verbally describe into a tape recorder what you see, or write it down on paper so you can remember it for your future visualization sessions.

Once you have created visualizations, you can put them to work for you by doing the workouts that follow.

AT A GLANCE

Constructing Affirmations and Visualizations

Step One Create your sacred space and get into a basic meditative state.

Step Two Take the goals, fears, and limiting beliefs you discovered earlier in this chapter and concentrate on them one by one, creating an affirming sentence that will free and empower you to receive the goals and release the fears and limiting beliefs.

Step Three Go on to visualizations, working with your goals to create detailed visual images. Write them down or describe them into a tape recorder.

Step Four Close your sacred space and write in your journal.

Using Your Affirmations and Visualizations

Once you have created affirmations and visualizations, there are several ways to use them. I have broken these down into easy-to-follow workout sessions. Try each one once, then choose those you like and keep doing them. You can do these in quickie sessions of three to five

minutes or longer sessions of ten to fifteen minutes, getting into a deep
state before every session. I suggest you spend a week on these workouts before moving on to chapter 4. Then add mini affirmation and visualization sessions to your weekly schedule as you move through the
rest of the book. This work has a cumulative effect; the more you do
it, the more you will see results.

As you do these sessions, concentrate on the phrase or mental image you have created and focus all your intention, all your psychic
power, to completely integrate that phrase or image into your life and
transform the words and pictures into real life experiences.

Affirmation and Visualization Workout 1

After you have created your sacred space and achieved a basic meditative state, choose one of the affirmations or visualizations you have
already created to work with. Close your eyes and repeat it in your
head over and over with intention and feeling. Let it fill your head; let
it inspire you. As you concentrate on it, imagine that it is an integral
part of your soul. Before you get bored with it, move on to a different
affirmation or visualization. Do what seems natural. Some days you
will spend two minutes on one, other days four minutes. End your session by closing your sacred space and write in your journal.

Affirmation and Visualization Workout 2

For this one you'll need a pen and paper. If you want to go all out, get
drawing materials like crayons, pastels, or markers. Create your sacred
space and get into a deep state. Pick an affirmation. Write it out on paper and say it verbally. You can write on lined paper, straight across the
lines if you want. Write big or small, make columns, make squiggly
doodles—whatever, just fill up a sheet of paper, back and front, saying

the affirmation over and over as you write. It doesn't matter what you do with these writings. If you're proud of them, you may hang them around your house or keep them somewhere. Or you may throw them away.

Visualizations are similar. Draw your visualization in great detail. Don't worry if you are not a master artist; you can always label the different items in your picture. When you are finished, hang these pictures up on your walls, mirrors, or closet doors.

Affirmation and Visualization Workout 3

You are going to make your very own affirmation and visualization tape, so get a tape recorder and a timer or stopwatch. Create your sacred space and get into a basic receptive state. Begin with a few affirmations. Turn on your tape recorder and repeat one affirmation slowly for thirty seconds. Do this with all the intention and feeling you can create. When the time is up, go on to another affirmation.

Turn the tape over and go on to visualizations. Close your eyes. Turn your recorder on and tape yourself verbally describing a visual image in great detail, calmly and slowly. Do all your visualizations the same way.

You can use the tape you've just made in many ways. Listen to it while you are driving, cleaning, commuting, sleeping, eating—even paying your taxes!

Affirmation and Visualization Workout 4

This is a meditative workout. Close your eyes and, as you breathe, use an affirmation as a mantra. A mantra is a repetitive statement meditators use to get into a deeper state ("Om" is the most common). You can say the words of your affirmation verbally, or even chant them.

Repeat the words rhythmically as you breathe in and out. Do this as long as you can stand the phrase and the sound of your voice. When you are bored, change the affirmation and the tone of your chant.

Although this repetition works best with affirmations, you can do this exercise with visualizations by closing your eyes and chanting a detailed description of your visualization to the rhythm of your breath.

Now you're finally ready to take your psychic ability and go for broke! In the next chapter, you'll learn to communicate with your angels. You'll be talking to your body and really exploring your psychic

Want Something You Don't Have? Write a Wish List!

Since you're putting in all this effort to develop your psychic intuition, you might as well use the ability to get things—lots of things—new jeans, a new VCR, a bigger apartment, more dates. Here's how.

Write out a short list of things you want. Spend a few moments reveling in these terrific items; think about what you will do with them once you get them and how much fun you will have. Keep the list close to you. Reread it often. You can even create a special workout session just to receive these items. Create your sacred space, get into a deep state, and describe with delight and detail each item, one by one. See them in your apartment, feel yourself wearing them.

Draw the items or cut them out from newspaper ads. You can even talk to the universe and provide a price, a time, and a date when you want to receive each item. Let the universe do its job. Miraculously, you'll see a sale or get a present, and one by one, you'll start actually receiving the things on your list.

I must say that there are two catches to this technique working well: One, you will receive only things that are within your comfort zone. If your wildest dream is a castle, you might want to shoot for a house and work your way up. Two, you will receive only things that are for your highest and greatest good. In other words, if you want something for the wrong reasons—it ain't coming to ya.

experiences. You'll learn how to get information on anything in your life that you want to know more about. There is no piece of information you cannot receive.

Now that you are free of anything that might limit your psychic development, you can go on to explore psychic energy to its fullest. All the exercise workouts in chapter 4 will enable you to become completely psychically aware. These are the exercises I did to develop my ability—and I still rely on them today. This stuff is so exciting that you may not want to stop doing psychic sessions.

Troubleshooting

Having a hard time taking a deeper look within? I know sometimes it's not easy to recognize things about yourself that aren't perfect, but in the long run it will help you develop your psychic ability and create the life you want to live. One of my clients said this was the toughest section he had to go through and the most life-altering, too. He found it so helpful that he kept asking for more.

Take your time. No one says that you have to do all your spring cleaning at once. Pace yourself and do only what you feel comfortable doing. If you get stuck on any of these workouts, move on to the next chapter and go back to it when you are ready. Believe me, you are going to change so much that you'll be ready before you know it.

chapter four

hold my calls, i'm levitating!

———

Quite frequently, my clients come to me with stories of psychic experiences they've had that they wish to understand better. They tell me about a dream they had the night before, for instance, or a vision they had when they were on the phone with a friend. It's great to be able to connect with psychic energy. But it's one thing to make contact with the universe and another to be able to interpret it and direct it to get the answers you want to live a better life.

Right now, you are at a big transition point in your development. You've already learned what psychic energy is and how to connect with it at will. You've worked on clearing your channel and making pure connections to psychic energy. In part II you're going to learn how to use psychic energy to change specific parts of your life. But first you need to know the easiest and most effective ways to get the information you need to create these changes. The exercises in this chapter are a bridge from the knowledge of universal energy you gained from the first half of the book to the practical application of that knowledge in the second half.

The six exercises in this chapter involve different conduits, or channels, geared to access different facets of psychic energy. Using these channels, you will always be able to get the most direct answers to whatever psychic questions you have. You can then bring this knowledge to the practical issues in part II and cure your headache, find your soulmate, or see when your next job opportunity will present itself.

The first conduit enables you to have direct contact with your universal helpers—your angels and spirit guides. The first workout, Having an Angel Party, allows you to become comfortable with your angels and spirit guides. Once you're comfortable accessing their energy, you will move on to the second exercise, Communicating with the Universe, in which you receive advice and wisdom directly from your heavenly helpers.

The next two exercises, Magnetizing Your Goals and Magnetizing Information, awaken the magnetic qualities of the universal energy within you, making you a magnet to attract and achieve your goals and receive any information you wish. Listening to Your Body, the fourth exercise, gives you access to all the information stored in the cells of your body, helping you to see and explore the experiences behind any blocked energy in your body, to understand the issues behind any blocks, and to clear them away to maintain good health.

The fifth workout, Finding Your Psychic Solution, is a way for you to use universal energy to search for answers to problems that are bothering you and to get rid of your worries and cares about any situation you may find yourself in. Finally, The Meaning Behind the Message is a way to explore your everyday psychic experiences and get the most possible information from them.

I have many clients and friends who do any one of these exercises depending on the situation they are in. My friend Jennifer communicates with the universe during her meditations to connect to her spirit guides. The information she receives helps her feel more grounded and empowered. My client Michelle does inner research to get the meaning behind the message when she wants to know more about her unusual psychic experiences. By understanding what the universe is telling her, she has a better handle on the lessons she is learning every day.

Do each of these exercises once or twice before moving on to the second half of this book. This will give you the understanding you need to make the concrete changes discussed in chapters 5, 6, and 7. You'll find yourself referring back to these exercises constantly as you discover the most practical ways to use them later in this book.

Ten Household Items That Are Actually Psychic Tools

One Radio. No matter what you are thinking, the song knows the answer.

Two Lawn mower. The loud grumble and constant vibrating can instantly recalibrate your inner senses.

Three Mirror. Stare into it until someone else stares back. This works best if you are sleep deprived.

Four Bowling ball. Covered up with a table cloth—it's an instant crystal ball. No one will know the difference.

Five Television. Stand in front of the fuzz at 4:00 A.M. If there are ghosts in your house, they'll suck you into the TV, where they feel you belong.

Six Dishwasher. Oops! Wrong list. That belongs on the household-items-that-cook-fish list.

Seven Sponges. It was recently discovered that sponges are actually ancient alien caca left here at the time of Atlantis.

Eight Frying pan. Always a good instrument for seeing stars.

Nine Telephone answering machine. Good for taking all those calls from the other side when you are off levitating.

Ten Coffee grounds. It works with tea leaves, and after all, this is the nineties.

Prepare to Party with the Universe

This first exercise will get you in contact with your universal helpers, allowing you to become comfortable with this energy. Before we begin to communicate with the other side in this exercise, let's discuss exactly what is over there. Your angels, spirit guides, and Higher Self are the primary assistants and communicators who can give you feedback from the universe.

Angels and spirit guides are very different beings with very different jobs, assignments, and origins. Therefore, there is a difference in the way their energy feels to you. This might sound strange now, but once you do this a few times, you'll begin to *know* the difference between them without having to get konked on the head with it.

Angels are sent to us by the universe to protect us and help us get what we want. They represent pure, unconditional love. Everything they do is dripping with happiness, joy, and lightness. When you connect with their energy, that is exactly what you feel.

Spirit guides, on the other hand, have been human before. They are souls who know exactly what we people are going through. Spirit guides contract with us to work together. It's a mutual choosing. They help us learn and grow; they help us get what we want, but they do it by teaching and guiding us. As they help us, they help themselves, because they, too, are learning and growing and evolving. They are completely devoted to us. They are our translators and intermediaries with the universe. Yet although their energy feels weightier, more grounded, spirit guides still have a huge sense of humor.

This next exercise is designed to help you to get used to sensing these differences while in the safe environment of your sacred space. One of my clients gets the heebie-jeebies every time he thinks about doing this. He can't quite get comfortable inviting these beings into his house and getting them to leave when it is all over. But before you get nervous, you should know that spirit guides and angels are around you anyway. They've been there since day one of your life. They assist and support us, but they will never interfere unless invited to do so. They will quietly support you until the day you say, "Help!" and then they step in. Since they are already there, when you have an angel party, all you are doing is inviting them to have a more conscious connection with you. And when you decide it's over, they go back to the quiet supportive position that they always have had. Oh, and don't worry about them sneaking up on your guests in your living room. When there's no party going on, they're too busy doing their job to scare anybody.

In addition to your angels and spirit guides, there are a few other beings on the other side with whom you can learn to consciously connect through this workout. God, for instance, or deceased relatives. If you want to experience a being other than your spirit guides or angels, make sure that you call in only beings who are for your highest and greatest good. In other words, this is not the time to find out about Satan. And stick to *your* deceased relatives, the ones you truly miss. This is not the appropriate time to try to talk to Marilyn Monroe or Elvis Presley. I do not believe in disturbing any soul at rest—unless you are an expert and this is your destiny. In that case, you need more practice before attempting it.

As you learn to sense the energy from your guides and angels, you will instinctively know when they are around. You'll begin to use your inner senses to see, hear, and feel them. You will begin to receive their messages and be able to use their guidance whenever you ask for it.

Psychic Workout
Angel Party!

This is a light and fun exercise designed for you to learn the differences among all the energies on the other side. It is a prelude to receiving deep communication with your guides and angels, which you will do in the next exercise. It is intended purely for fun, much as any party is—and, just like any other party, it is a great place to get to know the invited guests, have good conversation, and relax.

I love doing this workout on a lazy Sunday. I have a long writing session with my guides—which you will learn about in the next workout, Communicating with the Universe—and a relaxing angel party while I am in a warm bath. I combine a few of these exercises and do them for hours. I don't even realize how much time has gone by, and when it is all over I feel completely reenergized. (One of my clients says the only way she'll do this in a bath is to put on a bathing suit. OK, whatever suits your fancy. The angels don't care. If you feel you have to be fully clothed in order to do this, then skip the bath!)

The first step to having an angel party is to make up invitations. You can do this by writing to your guides or calling them in your mind and speaking directly to them. You can do this just moments before doing an angel party session, or you can invite them well in advance when you schedule your next session.

Write or say the following:

Dear Guides, Angels, Higher Self [God, Deceased Relatives]: I would like to invite you in for a special party now [or give time and date]. Only the energy from the purest source is invited for my highest and greatest good. Please attend in the manner that is most appropriate for me at this time. Thanks. Amen.

This invitation is just an example; you can get as creative as you want. The reason you invite your guides in the manner that is most appropriate for you *is so that they will show up in a way that you will like, and your experiences will always be within your comfort zone. This ensures that you won't have a negative experience at your own party.*

Begin, of course, by creating your sacred space. You've done this a thousand times, but this one will seem different, 'cause today you're having a party. If you choose to write an invitation rather than say it, place the writing on a shelf in full view until the day arrives, then use it to create your sacred space. Light your candles, recite your invocations. Have an extra moment of appreciation.

Sit down comfortably, close your eyes, and breathe deeply. Don't be surprised if you feel energy and start to get excited before you even really begin. After a few moments of concentrating on your breathing, you should be in a deep state of awareness. In your mind, create a funnel going from the crown of your head up and out into the universe. Mentally opening the funnel is like opening the front door of your house and letting in party guests. As you awaken your inner senses through your breathing, your guides will be hanging out on your doorstep waiting for you. You may perceive them in many different ways. You may see a flash of light or colors with your inner vision; you may hear or feel words, have chills, or just generally feel their presence with you in the room.

Keep breathing deeply, focusing your attention on the funnel. The first few times you do this exercise, you'll work on experimenting with feeling the different energies of your angels and spirit guides. Beginning with the angels, telepathically call to them, sending them a thought and asking them to surround you. Spend a few minutes breathing deeply, saturating yourself with their energy. Observe what you see, feel, and hear when you are surrounded by this energy.

When you are ready, move on to your spirit guides. Telepathically call to them, asking them to surround you. You may feel one, two, three—there is really no limit to the number of guides you have, but most people have one or two. You can feel their general presence or sense them standing or sitting near you in specific spots. Breathe deeply and enjoy their energy for a few moments, observing what you see, hear, and feel.

You can wind down and end your session here or go on to experience other energy from the other side. Call in God, or a deceased relative, and let the energy flow through you. When you are finished with your session, simply thank them all for coming, say goodbye, and shut off your funnel. Close your sacred space and write in your journal. Which group did you feel most comfortable with? Which one did you feel you connected to most easily and effortlessly?

Whenever you feel withdrawn or lonely, try a mini angel party. Give *yourself four to five minutes to sit in a comfortable place and verbally invite your guides to hang out with you. Open your funnel and let their energy revitalize you. You are never alone with your angels nearby.*

AT A GLANCE
Angel Party

Step One Send out invitations.

Step Two Create your sacred space and get into a deep state.

Step Three Create a funnel going from the crown of your head up and out into the universe. Open the funnel; your guides and angels will be sitting there waiting for you.

Step Four Telepathically call to your angels, asking them to surround you. Spend a few minutes breathing deeply, saturating yourself with their energy. Observe what you see, feel, and hear.

Step Five Move on to your spirit guides. Ask them to surround you. You may feel their general presence or feel them near you in specific spots. Observe what you see, hear, and feel.

Step Six End here, or go on to connect with God or a deceased relative.

Step Seven When you are finished with your session, simply thank these beings for coming, say goodbye, and shut off your funnel.

Step Eight Close your sacred space and write in your journal.

Communicating with Your Angels and Spirit Guides

As you know, your angels and guides are a very loving source of protection and guidance. They are your teachers and your greatest source of inspiration. By contacting them directly, you can get pages and pages of information for yourself and others. This will help you make better decisions and fulfill your destiny with grace and ease. You have already learned the difference between the energy of angels, spirit guides, and your Higher Self; the next step is to connect with them and get it all on paper.

My friend Miriam uses her computer to connect this way to the universe. She receives information, wisdom, and advice simply by typing "Dear God" on the keyboard, then asking a question. That is her best form of universal communication. The answers she gets this way are incredibly profound.

Talking to the universe, or to God, is an individual thing, and I prefer to connect with my angels when I want something and to my guides when I want to learn something. Personally, I feel that God is way too high up there to cultivate an intimate daily communication with, and since my guides are God's agents anyway, I have my intimate communications with my guides.

There are many ways you will feel this communication. You may see a series of pictures, or get hit with an instant understanding or insight. Once you have connected with the energy of your guides or angels, as you learned in the previous angel party exercise, you'll record what these beings have to say to you by describing what you see in your journal or on tape. The way most people receive this information is through a stream of words, as if they were taking dictation. Simply open to this flow and passively accept what you receive. Write it all down as fast as you can. Don't judge it, don't be too logical, and don't think too much, or you'll choke the flow. The faster you just write what you hear and feel, the faster the messages will come. You'll know you are receiving messages from your guides or angels because the dictation you receive will be in perfectly constructed sentences without any thought on your part whatever.

The most important thing you need to remember about this communication is trust. You will not know when the communications end or where they are going to take you. Just go with it. You may miss a few words when you first begin or get choppy sentences. This is perfectly normal. You are learning to tune in to the channel of spirit beings, and to get your thoughts out of their way. You'll see improvements every week. The more you do it, the deeper you will go.

There are so many gifted people who will find this type of communication extremely easy. Once you open up, you'll probably find a lot of messages awaiting pickup. Our guides have been on standby for a long time, so by the time we do this—whoosh! Out it flies.

Our guides and angels love getting information directly to us. It's their job. And when we reach out to receive it, we benefit all the more. The only thing you need to do to keep these messages flowing is to thank them often. Appreciation goes a long way.

One more thing . . . receiving information like this is great, but it is not gospel. Do not feel that this guidance is any more important than your own inner senses. Don't follow any information that doesn't resonate with you. Your choices are your own free will; guides and angels assist you with decision making, but they never take that power away from you.

Psychic Workout
Communicating with the Universe

Take out your journal and compose some important questions, leaving space for the answers. The more practical the question, the more practical the answer. Here are some good questions to ask:

What do I need to know right now?
What do I need to know about [an unresolved issue]?
What did I learn about [a past unresolved issue]?
What lessons am I working on right now?
Why did [a certain event or unresolved issue] happen to me?
How can I transcend this lesson or situation?

You can also ask your guides and angels their names, and physical descriptions, or explore the kind of relationship you have with them.

Create your sacred space and get into a basic receptive state. With your eyes closed, let your breathing relax into a deep, comfortable flow. In your third eye, or mind's eye, bring your attention to your first question. Invite your guides, angels, or Higher Self in to answer it. Let their energy flow through you. The answer will pop up immediately. After ten seconds or so, you'll be ready to write what you feel, hear, or see. You may feel that a certain area of your head is the center of this communication: your third eye, the spot just inside your ears, the middle of your head. If this is the case, it will help you to focus your concentration on that spot.

Write everything that comes to you in your journal. When the universe is done communicating, you will naturally stop writing. End your session by putting a protective shield of universal energy around you and close your sacred space. Reread the information when you are finished with your session. Then write about the experience in your journal.

AT A GLANCE
Communicating with the Universe

Step One Write the perfect question at the top of your journal.

Step Two Create your sacred space and get into a basic receptive state.

Step Three In your mind's eye, bring your attention to the question. Invite your guides, angels, or Higher Self in to answer it.

Step Four Let their energy and the answer flow through you. Write what you feel, hear, or see.

Step Five When they are finished dictating the answer to you, stop writing. End your session by putting a protective shield of universal energy around yourself and close your sacred space.

Step Six Reread the information you received and write about the experience in your journal.

Awakening Your Magnetic Self to Achieve
Goals and Receive Information

You are a channel for psychic energy. As this energy flows through you, it attracts to you what you focus on. Using psychic energy can enable you to literally use your body as a magnet to physically fulfill all your goals, wishes, and desires, as well as attract specific information and energy. Using your body as an anchor, you can miraculously find these things making their way to you.

I once magnetized into my life an old-fashioned seltzer bottle that I wanted to give my parents as a gift. For their anniversary, I thought it would be nice to make them old-fashioned egg creams—those very fifties New York drinks made from seltzer, milk, and chocolate syrup. I called many seltzer companies in search of a pressurized seltzer bottle for purchase, but had no luck. Then I spent some time magnetically visualizing exactly what I wanted, and one day, as I walked down a random street in Manhattan, I bumped into a guy carting seltzer bottles into an apartment building from the back of an unmarked van. He sold me a bottle on the spot.

You can use psychic magnetism either to attract fulfillment of your goals or to receive information. Part 1 of the following focuses on the former, part 2 on the latter. My friend Renato uses part 2. He gets into a deep meditative state and activates his magnetic qualities. He then asks what his next work opportunities will be. During his sessions, he clairvoyantly sees what job his magnetic ability is going to bring him next.

Psychic Workout
Magnetizing Your Goals

Before you begin, figure out what you want to magnetize into your life. Take out your list of goals and your wish list, from Setting Goals on page 66 and Wish List on page 76. Add anything you want: money, happiness, the perfect job, new shoes. There is nothing wrong or unspiritual about any of these things; you can use your new ability to mold this energy to get all these and more.

Once you have your list, create your sacred space and get into a basic meditative state. Imagine a cord going from the top of your head up into the universe. Pull down thick liquid white energy from the cord and fill your body with it as you breathe. Focus your attention on the energy's magnetic qualities. As you fill yourself with it, you are actually charging yourself with a powerful energy that will attract the things on your list like a magnet.

From the inside out, imagine your body glowing with this magnetic illumination. Take a moment to experience yourself as you possess this powerful attraction, and know that everything that serves your higher purpose is attracted to you. When you are ready, bring your attention to the first item on your list. Visualize the item making its way to you. In great detail, see the many ways it can come to you. Imagine yourself owning it and using it. Live it. Be it. Experience all the expansive feelings that go along with this owning, and verbally describe what's going on.

When you are finished, go on to the next item on your list. Spend as much time on a specific goal as you want; the most important thing is that you completely empower yourself to attract exactly what you want. End your session by surrounding yourself with a bubble of magnetic energy. Wear it all day.

Do this exercise in the morning, and see how differently people treat you throughout the day when you wear your coat of magnetic energy. Your friends and coworkers may not be able to pinpoint exactly what's up— new clothes? New makeup?

Magnetizing Your Goals

Step One Using your goals and wish lists from pages 66 and 76, write a short list of goals to magnetize.

Step Two Create your sacred space and get into a basic meditative state.

Step Three Create a cord going from the top of your head out into the universe.

Step Four Pull down the cord's thick liquid white energy and fill your body with it as you breathe. Imagine your body glowing with this magnetic illumination.

Step Five Bring your attention to the first goal on your list. Visualize all the ways it can come to you.

Step Six When you are finished, go on to the next item on your list.

Step Seven Surround yourself with a bubble of magnetic energy and wear it all day.

Psychic Workout
Magnetizing Information

Before you start your session, take a moment to think about the information you'd like to attract, whether it's information on your next job or relationship, your father's health, or your sister's pregnancy. Write your questions or topics in your journal and leave space for the answers. Do not do this exercise without a specific focal point in mind, or you'll receive hazy impressions, or no impressions at all, and that will just get you frustrated.

When you are ready to begin, create your sacred space and get into a basic meditative state. Create a cord going from the top of your head into the universe. Pull down the cord's thick liquid white energy and fill your body with it as you breathe. Focus your attention on the energy's magnetic qualities. As you fill yourself, you are actually charging yourself with a powerful energy that will attract information like a magnet. From the inside out, imagine your body glowing with this magnetic illumination. Take a moment to experience yourself as you possess this powerful attraction, and know that everything that serves your higher purpose is attracted to you.

When you are ready, bring your attention to the first question or topic on your list. See or feel the question in your mind's eye. Slowly repeat the question in your head a few times, as you concentrate deeply on it. Feel your body and mind attracting detailed answers to your question. Experience all the expansive feelings that go along with this process as you verbally describe what you see or write it down in your journal.

As you concentrate, leave space for the universe to answer you. If you are so focused on sending the question out that you leave no room to attract anything to you, you may not get an answer. When you have received all the details you feel you are going to get, move on to the next question or topic in your journal.

As I do this, I usually receive bits and pieces of information through my clairsentience and clairaudience. Together these pieces make up a total picture. Depending upon your natural bent, you'll be using any combination of abilities: clairvoyance, clairsentience, and clairaudience.

End your session by surrounding yourself with a bubble of magnetic energy and wear it all day.

AT A GLANCE
Magnetizing Information

Step One Write the questions for which you want answers.

Step Two Create your sacred space and get into a basic meditative state.

Step Three Create a cord going from the top of your head out into the universe.

Step Four Pull down the cord's thick liquid white energy and fill your body with it as you breathe. Imagine your body glowing with this magnetic illumination.

Step Five As you focus on your question, magnetically attract the answer and write it down.

Step Six When you are finished, go on to the next item on your list.

Step Seven Surround yourself with a bubble of magnetic energy and wear it all day.

Your Body Knows More Than You Think

Our bodies are like sponges. Every time we experience an emotion or a shocking event, it gets experienced with our physical bodies as well as with our minds. Just as our minds remember past experiences, so do our bodies. Our bodies are full of information from our present life, as well as our earlier ones, just waiting to be unlocked and decoded. We have physical scars because our bodies remember what happened in that spot years ago. We have so much intelligence locked up within our bodies that it is amazing what we could learn if we got in touch with those memories and that intelligence. This is not some *Mission: Impossible* scheme; all you have to do to get this information is know how to ask. That's where the following exercise comes in.

The first time I accessed knowledge within my body, a friend who was studying the healing art of reiki was practicing on me. I was lying in a relaxed state on her padded table. She started with my head and began to work toward my feet. After about ten minutes, she placed her hands on my stomach. Suddenly, part of me was in the Colosseum in Rome. I was a nineteen-year-old girl thrown to the lions for being Christian, and a big cat had torn out my guts in the exact area she touched. I know this sounds shocking, but it really wasn't. I actually laughed at this latent memory. No wonder I have a nervous stomach! Finally I understood why, for my whole life, I have been scared of cats.

As your body talks to you in this exercise, don't judge the information you receive. There is no reason for it *not* to be true. You will know that what your body is telling you is correct because, as your body releases its stories to you, it will also release its aches and pains.

Psychic Workout
Listening to Your Body

Write a list of major organs and muscle groups in your journal, leaving three lines to answer three questions that you will be asking yourself during this exercise. Begin by creating your sacred space and getting into a deep state. Take a few moments to get rhythmic breaths going. With your inner awareness, listen to your breathing.

Awaken your inner senses by bringing your attention to your skin. With your eyes closed, survey each area of your body from your toes to your head. Do your legs feel heavy on the couch? Does your belly feel hot? Your toes cold? Do you feel any area trying to get your attention? Note your observations. This should take about two minutes, after which you should be ready to go deeper. You can skip this warmup when you are more familiar with this exercise.

Survey your body again with your inner awareness, focusing on your muscles, bones, and organs. If you are a seeing person (clairvoyant), use a beam of inner light to scan your body slowly, seeing each area. If you are a hearing person (clairaudient), scan your body with an inner hearing aid that magnifies each spot as you focus on it. If you are a feeling person (clairsentient), scan your body with an inner sensing beam that feels the energy in each area.

Fully focus on one area at a time. Ask these questions about each area before moving to the next one. Record your response in your journal.

Is there any negative energy blocked here?
Are there any memories locked in here?
Is the energy balanced and flowing with this part of my body?

As you scan your body, trust the first response you feel. Concentrate on getting a yes or no answer the first time around. If you are naturally open, you may get some more details along with the yes or no answer. That's fine, but don't get off the scanning track to find out more. If you are a beginner, you'll stay more grounded by completing one step before going on to another.

After you have finished each muscle, bone, and organ on your list, make a new list of only those areas you found had energy blocked or contained stored memories. You can stop here and continue the rest of the exercise in another session. Or get back into a deep state and explore these areas now.

Bring your inner awareness to the first area on your list. Using your inner senses, get completely in harmony with the area. When you feel totally focused, ask these questions:

Why is there energy blocked here? Where did it originate from?
What memory is locked in here? Where did it originate from?

Your impressions may come to you in a color, a feeling, a series of words, or a sudden knowing; whatever they are, write them down, even if you are unsure whether they are correct. Our unconscious knows what it's doing, and first impressions are usually correct.

It may take you a few sessions to get through your body if you have a lot of blocked areas. As you unblock energy and unlock memories, you will feel your body working better and your fears disappearing. Release the negative energy and locked memories from the parts of the body you just explored by handing them, one by one, to your angels or sending them deep, deep into the earth. The earth will process it for you. Native Americans drain their negative energy into a small rock that they hold in the palm of their hands.

As you remove these blockages, it is important that you replace them with something better. Imagine pulling down from the universe pure white light energy, and send it into the areas you just cleared. You can do this visually or with words: "Dear Spirit, as I empty my body of negativity and trapped memories, I ask that your cleansing white light wash through these areas, clearing away any debris that might be left."

When you are ready to end your session, shrink your consciousness back into your body and create a protective shield of universal energy around you. Close your sacred space and write in your journal. After you have completed this exercise the first time, scan your body every so often to make sure you remain clear.

AT A GLANCE
Listening to Your Body

Step One Create your sacred space and get into a basic meditative state.

Step Two Awaken your inner senses by bringing your attention to your skin. With your eyes closed, survey each area of your body from your toes to your head as you breathe deeply.

Step Three Survey your body again, focusing on your muscles, bones, and organs. Ask these questions about each part:

Is there any negative energy blocked there?
Are there any memories locked in there?
Is the energy balanced and flowing with this part of my body?

Step Four Write down all the areas where there is blocked energy or stored memories. Choose a few places to explore and get back into a deep state.

Step Five Bring your inner awareness to the first area on your list. Using your inner senses, ask the following questions. Write down your impressions.

Why is this energy blocked? Where did it originate from?
What memory is locked here? Where did it originate from?

Step Six Before you end your session, release the unbalanced energy from the areas you just explored.

Step Seven Pull down pure white light energy and send it into the areas you just cleared. Do this visually or with words.

Step Eight Shrink your consciousness back into your body and create a protective shield of universal energy around yourself.

Step Nine Close your sacred space and write in your journal.

Got a Problem? Solve It Psychically!

As a budding psychic, there is no reason why you should be bothered by problems that you can easily find the answers to using the energy of the universe. Let's talk about what exactly a problem is. When something is bothering us, it's usually not the problem that bothers us, it's the unknown outcome or all the uncontrollable variables that are

The Universe Speaks Your Language, So Make Your Own Signals!

Our angels and spirit guides want to get their point across to us. And frankly, way up there they don't speak in what we consider languages; they only do that for our benefit. They are very smart characters, so it is quite easy for them to listen and speak to us in ways that we can completely understand. Tell your guides, out loud, during one of your sessions, how you'd like them to communicate with you. "Hey, guys, I like the wax to drip all over the floor," or "I'd like the propeller on my sacred beanie to spin." They'll use your signs to let you know they are around and that you are receiving their messages correctly.

getting on our nerves. When so much energy is wasted worrying about the outcomes of problems, we close ourselves into a box and can't see the situation clearly; then we can't perceive our best course of action. Next, we get panicky.

I'm sure you've experienced this at least once in your life. Use your psychic connection, and you will never operate like this again. By using your psychic ability at the onset of a problem, you will gain a general understanding of why something occurred, how it will resolve, and what your best course of action is. Knowing all this is quite comforting and will empower you to act freely and confidently.

Psychic Workout
Finding Your Psychic Solution

Take out your notebook and write a short description of anything that's really bothering you or anything you want to know more about, doing one unresolved issue per psychic session. What does your boss think of you? What's up with your budding relationship? How will your meeting with the IRS go? Next, write questions that are pertinent to your problem. If you're worried about something, you can ask:

What can I do to alleviate my stress over this?
How can I prevent this from occurring?
What are the best solutions?
How will this resolve?
What am I learning from this?
How did I get here to begin with?
What positive outcomes can occur from this?

If you want to know more about something, you can ask:

What do I need to know about this?
Why is this in my life?

What are the best actions for me to take regarding this?
How will this progress?

Choose three or four questions to ask in one session, and feel free to gear your questions to a specific topic. The best questions will get the best answers, so it is in your best interest to come up with some good ones. When you are ready, create your sacred space and get into a basic receptive state. As you breathe deeply, fill yourself with calming and balancing universal energy. Surround yourself with it, as if you are floating in a cloud or a bubble of universal energy. After a moment or two, you'll feel balanced and ready to begin.

With your eyes closed, awaken your inner senses (clairvoyance, clairaudience, clairsentience) as you did with the basic exercises in chapter 2. Concentrate on the first question; leave an opening of empty space in your head for receiving the answer as you wait for your Higher Self to answer you. It should only take moments for the answer to become apparent. You'll begin to see visual images, feel things, or hear streams of words. Start writing in your journal, and don't stop until the words or images stop coming to you.

Concentrate on another question and repeat the process. The answer to one question can bring about a whole new set of questions. When doing this exercise, you may discover either an end result or additional successful paths for you to take. You may ditch one of the questions you have already written in favor of asking questions you feel will give you the best answers.

End your session when you feel satisfied that you have received all the answers you are going to receive. Close your sacred space and reread your answers. Write down any additional information you may receive while rereading.

AT A GLANCE
Finding Your Psychic Solution

Step One Write a description of anything that's bothering you.

Step Two Compose questions that are pertinent to your issue.

Step Three Create your sacred space and get into a basic receptive state. Breathe deeply, and fill yourself with calming and balancing universal energy.

Step Four With your eyes closed, awaken your inner senses and concentrate on the first question. Write down the visual images, feelings, or sounds that you experience.

Step Five When you have finished picking up all you can on that particular question, repeat the process with your other questions.

Step Six End your session by closing your sacred space.

Step Seven Reread your answers and write down in your journal any additional information you may receive.

Researching Your Psychic Experiences

I had a very strange experience recently, and you know that if I thought it was strange, it must really be out there. I was eating lunch in a restaurant with a friend. While we were chatting, everything in my vision, my regular eyesight, became distorted, as if I were looking through some weird reflection like the little safety cameras on ATMs. I grabbed hold of the table to ground myself, as I tried to explain to my friend what exactly he looked like to me at the moment.

I could not explain what was going on, so as soon as I got home, I did this exercise. What I learned from the universe was that basically I had been looking at an overlapping picture of the current reality and a slightly future reality. That was why I saw distortions. The universe said that the stronger my ability grew, the more this would happen to me, and the more I would learn to control these abilities. Wow. I was definitely not expecting that—but it did make sense (to me!).

You, too, have had this kind of meaningful psychic experience, whether it was a feeling of déjà vu, an odd coincidence, or a precognitive dream. Your experience doesn't have to be as out there as mine to be worth investigating. Don't leave your psychic experiences unresearched! Delve into them to get the who, what, when, where, why, and how of your psychic messages. Every time you have an extraordinary experience, the universe is trying to teach you something about your life; it may be telling you something about your direction, the path you are on right now, or your destiny. If you don't explore these psychic happenings, you're missing out on valuable information.

When some people have psychic experiences, they think the meaning should be apparent right away. That is not always the case. If you want to know more, you may have to do research, just as you would go to a library if you wanted to gain knowledge.

Psychic events are not as easily understood as other events we experience daily. Often the symbols in a psychic dream or coincidence don't have a logical connection to reality. When you do the following exercise, you may not feel that the answers make sense. This is the way psychic symbols work; one reason to do this research is to gain deeper understanding through practice. Reviewing your notes after your session will make everything much more understandable.

Psychic Workout
The Meaning Behind the Message

Grab your notebook and write a brief description of a recent psychic experience you've had. Then list a few questions that pertain to that event. You can even break down all the elements of the event and ask for definitions of each one. Here are some basic things to ask:

Why did this occur?

Why was this other person/object involved?

What do I need to learn from this experience?

Is it related to a specific problem or event from last week?

What was this event trying to tell me?

Create your sacred space and get into a basic receptive state. Breathe deeply, with your eyes closed, and bring your inner attention to your third eye area. Imagine that area opening up inside your head, as if you are watching an inner TV set. The area of your forehead may feel hot. Through that opening, pull in psychic energy. Remember, this energy contains all the knowledge in the universe. Let it flow through you as your breath goes in and out.

When you feel relaxed and balanced, concentrate for a moment on the event you're investigating. Relive it briefly in your mind's eye as if watching it on your inner TV set. Once the energy of the event is activated, bring your attention to the first question on your list. Repeat the question in your head once or twice. As you pull in psychic energy, pull in the answer to the question. You will receive pictures (clairvoyance), have feelings (clairsentience), or hear words (clairaudience).

When you are finished, create a thick shield of protective universal energy around you, close your sacred space, and write in your journal.

AT A GLANCE
The Meaning Behind the Message

Step One Write a description of the psychic experience you want to investigate.

Step Two Compose a few questions that pertain to the event.

Step Three Create your sacred space and get into a basic receptive state.

Step Four Breathe deeply, with your eyes closed, and bring your inner attention to your third eye area. Imagine that area opening up inside your head. Through that opening, pull in psychic energy.

Step Five Concentrate on the event for a moment, reliving it briefly.

Step Six Bring your attention to the questions you're asking about the event. As you pull in psychic energy, pull in the answer to the question.

Step Seven End your session by creating a thick shield of protective universal energy, close your sacred space, and write in your journal.

There is one more thing you need to know before you are ready to use psychic energy to change your life—and that is how to properly use psychic energy and information. Good balanced psychics know how to separate themselves from the psychic information they receive. To get true, unbiased psychic answers, you have to be detached from them and not have any vested interest in the outcome. If you constantly focus on what you *want* the outcome to be, the power of your mind will taint your receptors.

For instance, if you want to know more about a guy you just started dating—but all you're thinking about is how you desperately want to marry him—you're closing yourself off to the truth. You may be with this guy for a certain amount of time, and learn and grow, and then a few years later marry another really great guy whom you love even more. Your psychic ability can help you learn lessons and avoid a bad breakup. But you will not get to those answers if you are still hung up on marrying the particular man in your present mind.

The universe communicates with you in the way that is best for you, but you may not be able to *predict* what that will be. You must let the universe communicate with you the way it wants to—without having any expectations. If you ask about this new guy in your life, you may *want* to hear all the specific things that will happen between the two of you, but the universe may give you a pretty story filled with metaphors instead. If the specific details are going to interfere with your growth, you won't get them. Or the universe may only give you information on the next step in your relationship and not the final outcome, so that you keep living in the present moment and not the future.

This happens more often when you are just starting to train your ability, because you learn these lessons early on in your psychic development. It can be very frustrating, I know, but you have to take baby steps before you can run a marathon. Remember, the universe has your best interests at heart. If you don't receive the answer you want, you will get the answer that is best for you at this time. Your psychic Higher Self knows more than you do; let it tell you what you need to know best about a particular situation so that you can act in the most empowered, balanced, and healthy manner.

Remember, there is always a reason why things happen the way they do—a lesson to be learned and a positive outcome behind *every* situation. The universe isn't here to hurt your feelings or withhold information. So if you ask a question and the first answer isn't what you want to hear and doesn't make you feel at peace, ask another question (a different question—not the same one over again) and look a little deeper until you are satisfied.

Connecting and communicating with the universe can be humbling. But receiving information from a source more evolved than ourselves does not mean we are any less worthy. We are co-creators with the universe. The fact that we humans are in a body does not mean we are any less powerful than our universal guides. It is an equal relationship. We are strong, powerful souls, not just weak physical beings. As you develop your connection to this source, you will also develop the ability to mold the universal energy and create the life you want. This balanced connection to psychic energy is our natural psychic state, and one we can only use when we are fully aware of its potential. This is the state you will use to transform every area of your life, to become the You you are meant to be.

Yahoo! You've just graduated from Psychic School 101! You're ready for the big time. In chapters 5, 6, and 7, you will put all this psychic energy to practical use. Here's where you'll learn to find your soulmate, lose ten pounds, become more popular, have better sales meetings, let go of lost love, get a great deal on a house—and become an all-around successful person.

You'll take all the skills that you have developed to access the universal energy and focus that energy in all areas of your life. You'll learn how to use the exercises you have already mastered in the most practical ways. You'll learn new workouts that will enable you to use psychic energy not only to get clear information but also to receive all sorts of other things . . . anything from those hard-to-find low-fat cookies to that old car you've been dreaming about—down to the exact year, make, and model. Through your ongoing connection to the universal energy, you will be empowered and inspired to fulfill your destiny. As an additional benefit of using your psychic connection, you will not only achieve your goals but also become a happier and more balanced person.

Troubleshooting
Want Assurance? Ask for a Sign!

This psychic business can be tough sometimes. No matter how good you are at this stuff, it's always good to get a pat on the back. Whenever you feel your trust and faith in your abilities wavering, stop what you are doing, close your eyes, and ask for some encouragement. I like to hum these words (to myself, of course): "Send me a miracle, give me a sign." No sooner said than done. Within moments, something crosses my path—on the TV show I am watching, in a magazine I am reading, outside my window—and I just know: "OK, that's my sign—thank you!"

Afraid of Going Too Far?

A lot of people are afraid to go all the way with their intuition. They are afraid that they are going to receive information that may overwhelm them, or pick up something they don't want to know. Or they fear that if they go in too deep they will change and become boring. I even believe that some people think if they go all the way, they may never come back! If you have any fears like this, it's time to let them go. You are not going to get any information you are not ready for, and you will never get an answer to a question you didn't ask. The universe is not in the habit of scaring or confusing its residents. If you are having a hard time letting go, it's not because you aren't meant to be psychic, it's because something is holding you back. Return to chapter 3 and do the Fears and Beliefs workout again, asking what your fears and beliefs are about your psychic ability. The answers should be very revealing!

part two

i want it, and i want it now

chapter five

love and relationships

P art II of this book is about manifesting your psychic abilities throughout the day. You'll be learning the most practical ways to use psychic energy to change your life for the better. You'll learn how to get into the psychic flow and let that flow guide your life. You'll get to know your true Self and reflect that self twenty-four hours a day, seven days a week. The universal energy knows what you want; it knows what you need. Trust it. By letting it reshape your life, you will gain the life you always wanted. By the time you are finished with this book, every area of your life will have had a psychic overhaul.

Let's look first at that all-important constant in our existence as human beings: our relationships with others. People matter to us: our bosses, our parents—and the most important love relationship—our soulmates or life partners. We want to create harmony and openness within all these relationships so that every day can be filled with love and support.

There are many occasions to use your psychic ability in relationships:

- *When you have just met someone*
- *When you are getting more serious*
- *When you are breaking up*
- *When you have a quarrel with your parents, friends, or siblings*
- *When you want to understand a loved one better*

We are constantly changing, growing, and evolving, and our relationships are constantly going through different stages as well. Whenever you enter into a new stage of relationship growth is a great time to look inside your psychic "crystal ball" for insights that will make the growth process clear to you.

By using your psychic ability to investigate these transitions, you can stay in a zone of deep knowing and understanding. You know your love life's path and lessons; every action and motivation is backed by pure universal energy. You naturally avoid pain and hurt by having a healthy understanding of the total picture and the positive outcome that is to be. You won't let yourself be caught up in anything that isn't on that path. And since you are connected to your truth, you will more easily find and keep true love.

Let me tell you what happens when two practicing intuitives come together in a relationship. This is a real life story! Renato came to me as a client, and we immediately became great friends. About a year after we met, he began dating Julia. Early on in their relationship he asked me what was going to happen between the two of them. I looked into it and said, "The two of you will be together for five to nine months, and then another man will come into her life. He is older and will be involved with her career. Although this will be a tough decision, she will end up with him."

Renato really cared for Julia, and he set out to figure out why they came together in the first place, and what he could do to change the

The Ten Best Psychic Pick-up Lines

One I'm a psychic, and I see me in your future.

Two I bet you're the kind of person who communicates with all the dogs as you walk down the street. Just think of me as a Labrador retriever.

Three If you want me to leave, blink, and I'll disappear!

Four What's a nice guy like you doing with karma like this?

Five Do you believe in telepathy? If you do, then you'll know what I'm thinking. . . . *So, what's it going to be, your place or mine?*

Six Are you levitating, or are you just happy to see me?

Seven I knew I was going to meet you—I've been waiting here for three lifetimes.

Eight Have you been sitting here long? Your aura is the color of a cool glass of zinfandel.

Nine Hey, you're kinda cute! Can I be your psychic friend?

Ten You're psychic? OK then, what's *my* sign?

outcome I foresaw. The two of them had a heart-to-heart talk, and Julia, who had done some psychic homework of her own, confessed her fear that somewhere along the line some other guy was going to come along and break them up. She was getting the same vibe I was.

Renato laid his love for Julia on the line. He told her that he had a lot of past lives to make up for, and that he was going to stay with her for as long as she wanted him. How romantic!! Within six months they were living together, and now they're engaged. Through Renato and Julia's conscientious psychic efforts, not only did they manage to change their destiny, but also they are so completely honest and deeply aware of each other's souls that they have one of the healthiest relationships I know. This, ladies and gentlemen, is why we do this psychic stuff.

You may be a skeptic and think, "Those original predictions must have been wrong in the first place." When two psychics say the same thing, that's not likely, but you can think anything you want. If you're a skeptic, there is nothing I could say to change your mind. The truth is that Renato and Julia's relationship is based on deeper psychic insights and inspirations. Their relationship is strong and bonded because of that shared information. And that holds true whether my and Julia's original predictions were accurate or not!

In the pages that follow, you'll learn how to put to practical use many of the exercises you've already learned to effect changes you wish to see in your love life and relationships. You will be able to use the Becoming Comfortable with Your Destiny exercise to visualize your soulmate; Finding Your Psychic Solution to get to the bottom of your relationship issues; and Affirmations and Visualizations to heal your relationship with your family.

This chapter also contains quick tips that will help you achieve your relationship goals with love partnership, family, and friends. You will be able to understand what your boyfriend or girlfriend is thinking about you; how your boss receives your work; and what your mother is wearing. You'll be able to access a visual image or feeling of what your next boyfriend or girlfriend looks like before he or she arrives in your life; you'll be able to find out exactly why you and your best friend are so close and why you've come into each other's life. If you can think of a love question or an unresolved relationship issue, the universe will provide the answer.

All You Need Is Love: Harmonizing Your Relationships

When any relationship in your life has problems, it's usually because the relationship has gone from a place of harmony to one of discord. Maybe there was a miscommunication. Perhaps you don't feel understood, or maybe old limiting patterns are showing themselves and creating a wedge in the relationship. No matter what the issue is, the bottom line is that you need to transcend the problem and get back to a place of harmony, where universal energy and love flows openly and freely.

When you use your psychic abilities in your love life—or in any relationship for that matter, including friends, siblings, parents, or coworkers—there are four major steps you need to follow in order to get into a deep flow of universal energy and achieve harmony. These are basic and practical steps that work every time—at the first hint of a problem in a new relationship, when you are newlyweds looking to buy a house, when you are raising children, when you have a falling out with your parents. Every time you feel that you have separated from the flow of unconditional love with those who are important to you, this process will bring you back.

The first step is to figure out the dynamics currently at work in the relationship that you're addressing, both positive and negative. If your relationship is not working, you need to understand the deeper picture and the actions and motivations behind this problem. You'll need to use a deep connection with the universe to find out what's keeping you from creating a bond of oneness with that person and to get beyond the specifics of your situation and the egos of all involved.

To do this, you can use any of the previous information-gathering exercises from chapter 4 (they're listed in the following exercise). To get the right answers and get to the bottom of a situation, you need to ask yourself some well-thought-out questions. Take a moment to really think about what you want to know, and formulate questions based on those needed insights. In the upcoming exercise I provide some good questions you can ask.

At the end of the last chapter, I stated that a good psychic is not attached to any one outcome. This is where that lesson comes into play. You cannot be afraid to see the truth as it really is, or you will not be able to see the issues as they really are. If you can't see underlying issues, you cannot fix the problem they are causing. Remember that there is always a positive outcome to every situation; looking for the reasons and the lessons behind a problem often makes the problem itself easier to look at.

After you have evaluated your relationship situation, the next step is to determine a path to the best possible outcome. Let the universe tell you what the best path for the relationship is at this time. Do this by getting into a meditative state and posing that question to yourself or the universe.

Once you have figured out where you should be going, the third phase of the process is to discover the appropriate action you can take to get yourself closer to that path. Do this by again using one of the information-gathering exercises from chapter 4 and asking yourself or the universe for the answer in a deep meditative state.

Finally, the last step in the process is to put that step into action. You may think that taking the action is the easy part—but NOOO!! Getting information is the easy part; it's integrating it into your life that takes real energy. This involves bringing unconscious habits out into the open, being aware of your intentions and motivations, breaking old patterns, and using the new action consistently. If you perform the exercises in this chapter with concerted effort and inner strength, you'll flow through your lessons with grace and get your relationship in harmony again.

Being honest with yourself is the most important part of this process. At any point during these four steps, you may decide that this effort is not doing you any good. There is nothing that says you are tied to a particular relationship. Just because you can bring your psychic ability to work on your relationship doesn't mean you have to do so. You may go through the first step in the process only to discover, when you review the dynamics of your relationship, that they are mostly negative. Or, when discovering your higher path during step 2, you may learn that you are better off without a certain person in your life. Then you will focus on an action toward a path to freedom and healing, instead of working to make the relationship work.

Psychic Workout
Achieving Harmony in Your Relationships

Take out your notebook. To figure out the dynamics currently at work in a particular relationship, first write out a series of questions that will get you the answers you desire. A few good ones are:

What are my deep thoughts and fears about this relationship?
What are (my friend/partner/sibling/parent's) deep thoughts and fears about this relationship?
What are the deeper dynamics at work here that created this issue?
Why did this issue come up at this time?
What was my role in creating this problem?
What was his/her role in creating this problem?

Choose the information-gathering exercise (from chapter 4) that works best for you:

- *Magnetizing Information*
- *Finding Your Psychic Solution*
- *Communicating with the Universe*

First, create your sacred space and use the exercise you chose to receive the answers to your questions.

Now that you have evaluated your situation, the second step is to determine a path to the best possible outcome. To do this, write the following questions in your notebook:

What is the path to the best possible outcome?
What path should this relationship be on?

Once again, get into a meditative state and use your favorite information-gathering exercise to receive answers to these questions.

The third step is discovering the next appropriate action you can take to get yourself closer to that higher path. If you wish, you can get the answer to this question at the same time you do the second step, since the two questions are related.

The final step is to take that action every day to bring yourself closer to the harmony you seek. Put all your intention and energy into transcending the problem. As you take the appropriate steps toward harmony and move forward toward your goal, repeat the third and fourth steps: learning an appropriate action, then taking it.

AT A GLANCE
Achieving Harmony in Your Relationships

Step One Write appropriate questions in your notebook regarding the dynamics at work in your relationship. Using any information-gathering exercise, get into a deep state and receive the answers to your questions.

Step Two Using the same procedure, ask for the path to the best possible outcome to your relationship problem. Write the answer down.

Step Three Again using the same procedure, discover the next appropriate action you can take to get yourself closer to that higher path.

Step Four Put the plan into action. With intention, follow the steps back to a place of harmony.

The Karma Connection

Love relationships contain some of the heaviest lessons in life. That's because our love relationships are woven around lessons we need to learn within ourselves and issues we have to work through with others. In even the best relationships, we can be carting around a lot of unresolved issues. Whether it's as simple as having too many expectations or as complex as being in the middle of a love triangle, every problem or unresolved issue that comes between two people is based on something called karma. When two people come together to learn and grow, it is karma that has brought them together.

Karma is a word that's thrown around a lot these days. In my definition, karma is what teaches us to act and react in a way that is for our highest and greatest good. Karma is the power behind the lessons that we each choose to work on and overcome in our lifetime. A relationship problem could come up in your life because you are reexperiencing something you messed up in a previous life, having to relive it again to correct the problem or unresolved issue. Or it can be something you are just working on for the first time. If you have a deep unresolved issue or problem, it is not really important to know where it originated. Either way, you are supposed to be learning to deal with it now, or it wouldn't be in your life at this moment.

Many people think in terms of good and bad karma. You may have heard someone say, "Oh, that's bad karma." But karma is not good or bad, it is the force that teaches us the difference between good and bad. If you once fired an employee at work for the wrong reasons, you may find yourself in the same situation twenty years later. The original action created the karma that you relived so many years later. You may look at the situation as negative, but by coming face to face with your original action, you learn from it. Karmic actions are often positive; you may buy a homeless person breakfast every day on your way to work, and that creates a positive situation that eventually brings positive rewards your way.

Have you ever had a relationship in which you loved another person deeply but couldn't seem to get beyond your defenses, no matter how hard you tried? Have you ever met someone and had so much in common that you both feel like you've known each other forever? Then you have experienced a karmic relationship. You can spot a *karmic relationship* by the power it has over you. There are also *karmic issues,* which you can spot by the difficulty you have learning from them and transcending them. Rocky relationships with parents and siblings are perfect examples of karmic relationships, and issues we experience every day, such as receiving respect from others, are examples of karmic issues. *Karmic situations* occur every day involving these relationships and unresolved issues: a dinner date, an encounter with a roommate, a business meeting.

Karma is a balancing act. Somewhere along the way, if unresolved karmic issues aren't addressed, they create an imbalance in your life or relationship. You need to learn the lesson underlying the karmic issue in order to correct the balance and continue the flow of universal energy. This is where your psychic ability comes into play. The only way you can understand the dynamics of this underlying karma is to use your ability to look into it on a deeper level. Once you understand that karma, you can use the power of universal energy to release issues and transcend it.

Sometimes we feel powerless against karmic issues or situations, but I assure you, if a certain problem is in our lives it is because on some level we feel strong enough to deal with it. The Achieving Harmony in Your Relationships exercise that you just learned will certainly help you get to know what you are dealing with, but the only way to really get control of these issues is to understand what karma is being played out and then work on releasing that karma.

Learning about all the underlying details that make up your karma (the karma you are currently dealing with) is just like investigating a psychic experience or finding a psychic solution. Therefore, you can use one of the exercises in chapter 4 to get the answers you are looking for, or you can even ask your spirit guides or angels.

Most important here are the questions you ask. In the next exercise I provide specific questions that you can ask to get to the bottom of the karma at work in your life. When you have the answers to these questions, you can begin to understand the lessons and issues that make up the karma. Knowledge can make all the difference. Knowing why you feel this way about someone or why that particular person is in your life will give you the power you need to operate in a balanced and healthy way.

In the first karma workout that follows, you will investigate your karmic relationships and issues. In the second and third workouts, you'll work on transcending those relationships and unresolved issues. A word of caution: You have to make sure you really want to release a situation before doing the second and third workouts, or they won't work. If you are in a situation that you don't want to let go of, be honest with yourself. Understanding the karma and releasing the karma are two entirely different things. You can completely understand the who, what, when, where, and why of a situation and still not be prepared to work through it. That's OK—give yourself time. You'll work on releasing it whenever you're ready.

Whenever you are ready to release the karma that surrounds you, do one of the two transcending karma workouts. The first is geared toward releasing karmic relationships, such as those with your friends, family members, or spouse. The second focuses on karmic issues that get in the way of your relationships, such as financial responsibilities within your marriage, judgment issues between you and your parents, or a fear of intimacy that keeps you apart from your boyfriend/girlfriend. Very often relationships and unresolved issues are intertwined; feel free to do both transcending karma exercises, one to release the person you are involved with, and one to transcend the issue you are working on. They work well together.

Psychic Workout
Understanding Karma

The first part of transcending karma is knowing what you are dealing with. To do that, first write a short description in your notebook of an issue or relationship that's bothering you, then write a series of questions geared to getting at the dynamics behind the problem. Some good questions are:

What is the karma between me and my partner, friend, sibling?
What do I have to learn from this person?
What is this person learning from me?
Why were we brought together at this time?
Where did this karma originate?

Choose one of the following information-gathering exercises in chapter 4:

- *Magnetizing Information*
- *Finding Your Psychic Solution*
- *The Meaning Behind the Message*
- *Communicating with the Universe*

Create your sacred space, get into a meditative state, and use the exercise you chose to get the answers to your questions. Write them in your journal. End your session as instructed.

Give yourself a moment to separate from the information, then reread your notes. Once you fully understand the karma, you can use that knowledge to release it in either of the following exercises.

AT A GLANCE
Understanding Karma

Step One Write a brief description of the karmic issue that you wish to look into, as well as a series of questions to ask the universe.

Step Two Create your sacred space and get into a meditative state.

Step Three Use one of the information-gathering exercises from chapter 4 to receive the answers to your questions. Write them down.

Step Four End your session, close your sacred space, and reread your notes.

Psychic Workout
Transcending Karmic Relationships

This exercise is designed to separate you from the limitations you may be experiencing in a particular relationship, and heal the wounds. Remember the affirmations and visualizations you did in chapter 3? This exercise works in a similar way, through repetition. Either create your sacred space before doing this workout, or simply light a candle. Repetition is the key, and you'll be doing this three to five times a day in order for it to be effective, so after a while, you'll probably find that creating a sacred space is distracting.

To begin, sit, stand, or lie down with your eyes closed, and breathe deeply and fully. In your mind's eye, create a ball of light three to four feet above your head, and a few feet in front of you, so that you have it comfortably in your sight without having to bend your neck too far back. This ball of light is the purest source of universal energy—your angels, spirit guides, Higher Self, or God.

This should take no more than fifteen to thirty seconds. When you are ready, repeat the following statement a few times, feeling it with all of your being:

Dear Spirit, I release [name of person] to you. Please balance the karma between us. Heal this relationship and make it what it is meant to be, as quickly as possible. Thank you.

As you repeat this phrase, focus on the person or relationship troubling you and visualize yourself handing that relationship to the ball of light. Release the relationship and let it float up to the light. Let the universe fix the relationship and return it whole. Don't worry about how or when, just do the releasing part. Repeat this process for a few days (maybe even weeks, if it's a toughie) until you feel a better balance in your relationship.

The more you say this phrase, the faster and more effectively it will work. Feel free to do this exercise wherever and whenever you have twenty to thirty seconds to spare: during your commute, during your lunch break, on line at the bank, while stuck in traffic.

This is a great exercise for healing a bad breakup or a quarrel with a friend or family member.

AT A GLANCE
Transcending Karmic Relationships

Step One Sit, stand, or lie down with your eyes closed, and breathe deeply.

Step Two In your mind's eye, create a ball of light three to four feet above your head and a few feet in front of you. This is the purest source in the universe.

Step Three As you repeat the words below, focus on a relationship/ person and visualize yourself handing that relationship/person to the ball of light:

Dear Spirit, I release [name of person] to you. Please balance the karma between us. Heal this relationship and make it what it is meant to be, as quickly as possible. Thank you.

Psychic Workout
Transcending Karmic Issues and Situations

This exercise is designed to help you transcend unresolved issues and daily situations that can get in the way of experiencing the flow of universal energy. As with the previous exercise, this works through repetition.

To begin, sit, stand, or lie down with your eyes closed and breathe deeply. Create a ball of light three to four feet above your head, and a few feet in front of you, so that it is comfortably in your sight without your hav-

ing to bend your neck too far back. This ball of light is the purest source of universal energy—your angels, spirit guides, Higher Self, or God.

This should take no more than fifteen to thirty seconds. When you are ready, repeat the following statement a few times, feeling it with all of your being.

> Dear Spirit, I release [issue or situation] to you. Please balance the karma within it. Heal it, and provide an outcome that is for the greater good of all involved. Make it what it is meant to be, as quickly as possible. Thank you.

As you repeat this phrase, visualize yourself handing the unresolved issue you are focusing on to the universe. Release it and let it float up to the ball of light. Let the universe fix the issue or situation and return it whole. Don't worry about how or when, just do the releasing part.

The more you say this phrase, the better it works. Feel free to do this exercise wherever and whenever you have thirty seconds to spare.

AT A GLANCE
Transcending Karmic Issues and Situations

Step One Sit, stand, or lie down with your eyes closed, and breathe deeply.

Step Two In your mind's eye, create a ball of light three to four feet above your head and a few feet in front of you. This is the purest source in the universe.

Step Three As you repeat the words below, focus on an issue or situation and visualize yourself handing it to the ball of light:

> Dear Spirit, I release [issue or situation] to you. Please balance the karma within it. Heal it, and provide an outcome that is for the greater good of all involved. Make it what it is meant to be, as quickly as possible. Thank you.

Transcending Relationship Problems with Forgiveness

In addition to karma, another thing that can choke your ability to give and receive love is the lack of forgiveness. We're in countless relationships over the course of a lifetime—with parents, neighbors, friends, lovers—and every day we are in these relationships we are learning and growing. Within these situations we act and react. We might not always agree with another person, and we might not always approve. But if we hold on to that disapproval—or anger, shame, or judgment against another—we stop learning, growing, and moving through the different stages of our unique life path. These negative emotions stop us from really connecting to the love we deserve from all our relationships and keep us isolated and alone. They clog the flow of psychic energy in your life. In other words, if you have recently had a negative situation or are currently in one, in order to get beyond it you must forgive yourself and the other person.

It doesn't matter which end of the situation you are on—the aggressor or the agressee—you still have to forgive to get beyond the negativity. When I say forgive someone, I don't mean that if you've been treated harshly you should forgive a person and *go back to an*

Approach Someone, the Angelic Way

Are you interested in someone but don't know how to approach him or her? Let your guides and angels do it for you. The next time you have a quiet moment, call to your spirit guides and angels. Visualize the person and ask your angels and guides to talk to his or her angels and guides. Tell them that you like this person and would like this person to know that you are interested in starting a friendship with them (maybe even something more!). Do this every day for a week or two. Then keep on the lookout—if you have increased contact with the person, or the person approaches you, you know that they got your message. Stay tuned!

unchanged relationship. I mean that by holding on to the anger, pain, or judgment you have involving this person—no matter how justified it is—you limit yourself and your capacity to love again. As you forgive, you will again flow with psychic energy. It is then your choice to stay, leave, or change the relationship.

Whether you are currently in a committed relationship or are getting over a bad one, this is not easy, but either way, it must be done in order to continue the flow of love in your life. There is a simple forgiveness exercise that will work wonders to help your relationship transcend this limitation. It will also help you get over a bad breakup.

You can do this exercise to forgive yourself as well. We are sometimes our own harshest critics, and holding on to pain or anger—even if it's directed back at you—doesn't help anybody.

This following exercise is very similar to the preceding ones. It works by way of repetition—as often as five times a day or more. Do it on the subway, in your car, during your bike ride, or in the shower.

Psychic Workout
Forgiveness

Begin by closing your eyes and breathing deeply and fully. Create a ball of light three to four feet above your head and a few feet in front of you. Make sure that it is comfortably in your sight without having to bend your neck too far back. This ball of light is the purest source of universal energy— your angels, spirit guides, Higher Self, or God. This should take no more than fifteen to thirty seconds.

When you are ready, repeat the following statement a few times, feeling it with all of your being:

Dear [name of person], I forgive you for your imperfections as I forgive myself for mine. I forgive you and release you. I release the [anger, pain, judgment, etc.] I have against you. I release you to be exactly who you are. With that I am free.

As you repeat this phrase, visualize yourself handing that person to the universe. Release the image and let it float up to the light.

AT   A   GLANCE
Forgiveness

Step One Begin by closing your eyes and breathing deeply and fully.

Step Two Create a ball of light three to four feet above your head and a few feet in front of you. This ball of light is the purest source of universal energy. This should take fifteen to thirty seconds.

Step Three Repeat the following statement several times, feeling it with all of your being:

Dear [name of person], I forgive you for your imperfections as I forgive myself for mine. I forgive you and release you. I release the [anger, pain, judgment, etc.] I have against you. I release you to be exactly who you are. With that I am free.

Step Four As you repeat this phrase, visualize yourself handing that person to the universe. Release the image and let it float up to the light.

What about All Those Other Relationship Issues?

Often our relationship issues are complex and confusing, and they don't fit exactly into the harmonizing, karma, or forgiveness exercises that we have just done. Do you find yourself afraid to express yourself in your relationships? Do you always seem to fall in love with people who are terrible for you? Are you eager to find a new relationship but

Psychic Socializing

Before your next date or party, do some psychic socializing! Take out your note-book and write a short description of the coming event along with the date on which it is taking place. Getting into a meditative state, bring yourself to the future event and ask yourself what is going to happen. Can you hear what you're going to talk about? Can you see what your friends are wearing? Write down what you see, hear, and feel. Then, throughout the event itself, see how close you came in your psychic session to the real event. Keep doing this—it will get a lot easier, and you'll get better at it each time.

can't quite get over being hurt by your last romance? If any of these examples ring true for you, then you need what follows!

These exercises and tips will help you deal with all the leftover issues that can get in the way of a successful and fulfilled love life: getting over your resistance and fears, finding true love, picking the right partner, and getting over lost love. These exercises will enable you to clear your slate so that you can have the love in your life that you deserve.

Getting over Resistance, Fears, and Other Human Hangups

When it comes to love, we humans can be very weak—and I write that with all sincerity. I know personally that as strong as I am in other aspects of my life, I can get too carried away when it comes to love. And if you're like me, when this happens, every step of the way you're completely aware of what you are doing. You know it's not good, but you do it anyway. Sometimes it is just not that easy to take the high road.

We know we're better off speaking the truth in our relationships, but sometimes we're afraid of hurting our mate's feelings. We don't want to break up with someone even though we know the relationship is a bad one. We're afraid to speak up for fear that our partner will leave us. The list goes on and on.

Learning lessons isn't always easy. Understanding an issue intellectually is very different from putting that understanding into action every day. So what do you do when you desperately want to fix your relationship, yet something is holding you back from following the path? You find that the solution you know is right isn't working? Or every time you try taking appropriate actions, you mess up? As soon as you notice a pattern in the way of your healing, don't become frustrated and guiltridden or give up. Instead, turn the pattern into a constructive learning tool.

Let me tell you about my client Danielle. She was having problems with her ex-husband. She was trying to have a friendly relationship with him for their child's sake, but he was continually putting her in the middle of his relationship with his current wife. No matter what action she seemed to take, she somehow ended up feeling hurt and manipulated. Then she did this exercise, and she discovered the underlying reasons for their inability to let go of this bizarre relationship and what actions she needed to take to fix the problems. The universe gave her the understanding she needed to operate within her full power. Now she is taking the appropriate actions as well as doing the exercises in transcending karma, and she is on her way to transcending the problems.

When you're continually having a problem taking action, or whatever action you are taking is constantly ineffective, your unconscious is trying to tell you something. By going within and looking into these negative patterns, you give them space to talk to you. You'll discover the reasons that are causing them—and the ways you can get around them or eliminate them altogether.

Sometimes these reasons are so unconscious and invisible that we cannot spot them without doing inner investigation. Using the Fears and Beliefs exercise from chapter 3, and/or any of the information-gathering exercises from chapter 4, you can access the fears, beliefs, motivations, and any other relevant issues behind these slip-ups.

Once you understand the fears and beliefs behind your resistance, you can begin to release these motivations. With the help of other exercises in chapters 3 and 4 you can transcend your limiting actions and get back on a path to love and harmony.

Psychic Workout
Discovering and Releasing Your Resistance to Love

Take out your notebook. Before you begin, write a brief description of the incident or event in which you feel your resistance or fear of love comes into play. Write these questions in your notebook, leaving space for the answers:

What are my fears about this path or action?
What are my beliefs about this path or action?
What is the reason behind my resistance?

Take out the instructions for the Fears and Beliefs workout in chapter 3 or any of the information-gathering exercises from chapter 4 (Communicating with the Universe, Finding Your Psychic Solution, or Magnetizing Your Goals). Begin by creating your sacred space and getting into a meditative state. Follow the directions for the exercise you chose and get the answers to your questions.

Take a moment to reflect on your answers. Once you know the underlying reasons for your resistance, get back into a meditative state to find out what steps and actions you can take to release the resistance and find the love you deserve. Here are some good questions you can ask:

How can I find happiness within my relationships?
What are the best actions I can take to create a fulfilling relationship?
How can I best release the fears and negative beliefs that I have about love?

The steps you take should also include other exercises in this book. Visualize yourself free from restriction in the Becoming Comfortable with Your Destiny workout from chapter 3. Do Affirmations and Visualizations (chapter 3) to help you release the resistance. And use Magnetizing Your Goals (chapter 4) to attract a complete You, free from any restrictions on your love life.

AT A GLANCE
Discovering and Releasing Your Resistance to Love

Step One Write appropriate questions in your notebook.

Step Two Do the Fears and Beliefs workout or any of the information-gathering exercises from chapter 4 to receive answers to those questions.

Step Three Do the exercise again to learn the steps you can take to release the resistance.

Step Four Take the steps. Include these weekly psychic workouts: Becoming Comfortable with Your Destiny, Magnetizing Your Goals, and Constructing Affirmations and Visualizations.

Getting Over Lost Love

Love is such an important part of our lives that when we are in a good relationship, we feel transformed. And ending a relationship or getting over a bad relationship can be one of the most difficult periods of our lives. Psychic ability can't necessarily prevent a breakup, but it can soften the blow and make recovery easier and quicker.

Whenever you are feeling down, sad, or depressed, instead of wallowing in that sorrow, look at those feelings as constructive tools to find your happiness. When I say that I don't mean that you should deny them. Don't push them under the rug and pretend you're happy. Instead, give yourself time to express those feelings while you simultaneously plan a future time when you will put them aside and talk to the universe. In order to use your despairing feelings as answer-giving tools, you do have to put those feelings on hold at a certain point or else your answers will only reflect that despair.

The rule is that you are free to wallow as much as you want up until your scheduled session; then you will put all the negative emotions aside and do your psychic workout, not being attached to any answers you may get during that session. It may help to remind yourself that this is only for fifteen minutes, and that you may continue to wallow when you are finished with this exercise (although you may not want to after doing this healing work).

As you do the exercise and receive your answers, the universal energy that you are connecting to will also rebalance your energy. When you are finished with your session, you will feel calm and refreshed, and you may not want to wallow in your sorrow anymore.

Unfortunately, just receiving answers to your questions isn't an easy out. You are still going to be left with your feelings of loss, anger, and depression, which you'll have to release so that you can move on to find a new healthy relationship. That is where the exercises earlier in this chapter come in handy. Do the workouts in transcending karma and the Forgiveness workout over and over again. Also do some of the exercises in chapter 8 and the Rebalance Your Energy, Restore Your Health workout in chapter 7.

The more you work at releasing the limiting and painful feelings from a breakup, the more quickly you will heal, and the sooner you will be able to go on to the fulfilling relationship you are meant to have.

Psychic Workout
Getting Over Lost Love

Schedule a time in advance to do a session. When that time comes, take out your notebook and write several questions geared toward understanding your pain. Some good questions are:

What do I need to learn from this situation?
Why do I feel this way?
Why did this occur?
When am I going to feel better?
Tell me about my next love opportunity.

Choose one of the following information-gathering exercises from chapter 4:

- *Communicating with the Universe*
- *Finding Your Psychic Solution*
- *Magnetizing Information*

Create your sacred space and take several deep breaths. As you inhale and exhale, focus on letting go of any negative emotions. Breathe in pure energy, breathe out negativity. When you are calm, go through the steps of the exercise and receive the answers to your questions. As you do so, the psychic energy that you are connecting to will also rebalance your internal energy.

Get back into a meditative state to learn appropriate actions you can take that will help you get over your lost love. Write the following question in your notebook:

What can I do to get over this?

Again create your sacred space and receive the answer to the question. Then take the steps. Once you understand the issues that you are working on and the steps you can take to alleviate this pain, reread chapter 8 and add any exercises you feel are appropriate, as well as adding these psychic workouts to your day:

Transcending Karmic Relationships
Transcending Karmic Issues and Situations
Forgiveness
Rebalance Your Energy, Restore Your Health (chapter 7)

AT A GLANCE
Getting Over Lost Love

Step One Take out your notebook and write down appropriate questions.

Step Two Choose one of the information-gathering exercises from chapter 4.

Step Three Take several deep breaths. As you inhale and exhale, focus on letting go of negative emotions. Breathe in pure energy, breathe out negativity.

Step Four Do the exercise and receive your answers.

Step Five To discover appropriate actions, get back into a meditative state and ask the universe what to do.

Step Six Take these steps, and do the additional psychic workouts just listed.

Leave the Wrong Ones, Pick the Right Ones!

OK, so you don't have problems attracting relationships, but no matter who you get involved with, that person always turns out to be Mr. or Ms. Wrong. Think this is out of your control? Think again.

The reason we attract certain types of people into our lives is because we are learning to overcome specific issues that these people bring up in our relationships with them. Let's say you need to learn to speak your mind freely. Well, chances are you are going to attract someone into your life who may be inclined to speak for you unless you speak up. If you need to learn to make your own decisions, you may find yourself with a partner who makes the wrong decisions for you. Once you address the issue within you, the problem in the relationship goes away. This can happen in all your relationships, including those with your parents, siblings, and friends.

Every relationship we have teaches us something. Most of the time we are unaware that learning is occurring, unless we consciously think about it. Think back to your previous bad relationships. Were there a few consistent problems that brought out some weakness within either you or your partner? What about your good relationships of the past? Were there some continual problems that brought about growth and a positive change in your behavior?

Going through these relationships is never easy; often we don't notice there is a problem until a pattern has been repeated many times. When we break up with a person without overcoming the lesson we're meant to learn from him or her, we attract a similar relationship again in order to take another shot at the problem. Breaking up can be like running away from the problem. Without figuring out why this pattern is in your life, you will never transcend the issues and attract Mr. or Ms. Right.

There is no need to endlessly repeat a bad pattern. By looking into your past bad relationships and finding the unresolved issues within them, you can use the universal energy to transcend them. Once you have learned the lesson, you will never attract that type of person again. It's that simple.

Once you know the underlying reasons for these issues, you can begin to eliminate them from your life. You can do that in several ways. One way is by taking the appropriate action and the other way is to use the psychic energy of your workout sessions.

After you've eliminated these issues, it is likely that you'll run into a lukewarm version of them in your next relationship. Not because the universe wants to give you heartburn, but just to make sure you learned the lesson correctly. When you spot the old pattern, handle the situation with your new knowledge. The pattern will be forever broken, and you'll go on to find romantic bliss!

Psychic Workout
Never Attract Mr. or Ms. Wrong Again!

Take out your notebook and write a brief description of an issue that came up in a past or current relationship (one issue per session). Then write a series of questions geared to dissect the issue and discover the pattern underlying it. Here are some good ones:

What are/were my limiting patterns in this relationship?
What lessons am I supposed to learn from this person?
What is the reason I attracted this person into my life?
What were/are the dynamics that caused this problem in this relationship?

Choose one of the following information-gathering exercises from chapter 4:

- *Communicating with the Universe*
- *Finding Your Psychic Solution*
- *Magnetizing Your Goals*
- *Magnetizing Information*

Create your sacred space, get into a meditative state, and receive the answers to your questions.

The next step is to eliminate the unresolved issues from your life using positive actions and the added power of psychic workouts. To discover the appropriate actions, use an information-gathering exercise and ask the universe these questions:

What can I do to overcome this issue?

What is the next appropriate action for me to take to eliminate this problem from my life?

End your session as instructed. To add psychic oomph to the action, do Becoming Comfortable with Your Destiny, visualizing the perfect You with all the characteristics you are currently learning. Create a list of affirmations (chapter 3) that counterbalance the unresolved issue, and visualize yourself dealing with the issue appropriately in all of your relationships. Do the Magnetizing Your Goals workout (chapter 4), imagining yourself handling the issue well in all your relationships.

AT A GLANCE
Never Attract Mr. or Ms. Wrong Again!

Step One Take out your notebook and write a brief description of an issue you experienced in a past or current relationship (one issue per session).

Step Two Write a series of questions geared to dissect the issue and discover the pattern.

Step Three Choose one of the information-gathering exercises from chapter 4 and receive the answers to your questions.

Step Four To discover the appropriate actions, get back into a meditative state and ask the universe the two questions listed above.

Step Five To add psychic oomph to the action, do the mini exercises and workouts just listed.

Finding True Love

One of the most popular questions my clients ask in my private consultations is, "When am I going to find my soulmate?" This is one of our most important desires. When we are in love, we naturally access universal or psychic energy and share that connection with all those we come in contact with. When we do not have love in our lives, many of us feel sad or lonely, and that is because our natural connection to those inspired feelings of love and oneness is shut off.

If you do not have love in your life, there may be a few reasons. It's possible that at this time the universe is telling you that you need to be alone in order to learn certain lessons. Alternatively, you may be holding onto negative fears and/or beliefs that are keeping you from experiencing true love. Perhaps on some level, conscious or unconscious, you made a choice not to become involved in a love relationship right now. Or maybe the person you are slated to have a relationship with is not yet ready to meet you.

There are four different ways of handling a lack of love in your life, depending on which of these circumstances sound most like you. To discover what category you fit into, choose one of the information-gathering exercises from chapter 4 and ask yourself or your spirit guides, "Why don't I have love in my life at this time?" The answer should fit into one, two, even three of the four categories just stated.

If you fit into the first category, *at this time, you need to be alone to learn the lessons you are currently dealing with in your life.* You need to do more inner research to figure out what lessons you are meant to be learning. Once you learn those lessons, you are free to find love. In addition, we know that the busier you are and the more fulfilled you become, the less you will feel that you are missing something in your life. Your destiny is exciting. If you discover what lessons you are learning at this time, you can go full steam ahead into your future and meet your destiny. As you go through life learning lessons, at the time that is best you will connect with your soulmate and have a great relationship.

If you find yourself in the second category, *you are holding on to some negative fears and/or beliefs that stop you from experiencing true love.* Your challenge is to work on getting rid of those limitations. Go to the section in this chapter that deals with getting over resistance and fears (page 127); then use the Becoming Comfortable with Your Destiny exercise (chapter 3) to focus on your new comfort with true love. Construct the perfect Affirmations and Visualizations (chapter 3) that will enable you to get what you want—true love. Free yourself from negativity, and you will free yourself to find the love you are meant to have.

If you fit into the third category, *you have made a choice not to become involved in a love relationship right now.* Chances are you don't feel as though you need a relationship as much as some other people you know. You may feel as though you want a romantic partner, but you're not really experiencing feelings of loneliness. People who make this choice, whether it is conscious or unconscious, have a take-it-or-leave-it attitude when it comes to their love lives, and they usually end up having relationships that are casual or noncommitted. If you fall into that group and you want a deep, committed relationship, you must make the decision that a relationship is important to you now and focus your intention on creating the perfect mate. You can do that through affirmations and visualizations as well as through the goal exercises in chapter 3 and the exercises on magnetizing your goals and information in chapter 4.

Finally, if you discovered you fit into the fourth category, *the person you are slated to have a relationship with is not ready to meet you,* then you just have to wait! As they say, patience is a virtue—and it is also one of the most common of life's lessons. While you're waiting, you can continue to ask the universe more questions and thereby help your destiny along.

Create a Relationship Journal

If you and your partner, friend, or family member are into having a psychic relationship—one in which both of you use your abilities to understand your relationship, as Renato and Julia do—you can start a special journal on the subject. Every week, do one or two psychic sessions dedicated to your relationship. Choose any of the exercises in this book and ask whatever questions are relevant to the two of you: What lessons are we working on together? What am I learning from my partner? Do we have past lives together?

When I first started talking to the universe on a regular basis, I started a relationship journal without the knowledge of my now ex-boyfriend Jeff. It really helped me develop my ability to hear the universe. Every day without fail I logged in another entry. He and I had a lot of heavy, unresolved karmic issues with each other, which having this journal helped me understand. One day, I took a risk and gave him a copy of the journal. It was the best thing I ever did for both of us. No matter how resistant he initially was when I handed him that thick diary, truth speaks its own language. He read it and reread it several times, and, though we weren't meant to be together, it helped us get through our breakup. And we remain good friends today.

Here's one of my diary entries:

The insights you both have are prepared on different scales. Accepting differences without attack is the best form of friendship. The way to achieve this is to let go of judgments against one another and to allow yourselves to understand both sides of the issue. You, Stacey, should not be afraid of expressing who you are out of fear of rejection. And Jeff needs to see his point of view is not ignored if it remains opposed. If either of you feels the need to be right, the other is automatically wrong. Let go of the concepts of right and wrong and there will be no need to prove your opinions to be correct or appropriate. It's OK not to be perfect.

Expressing Oneness and Unconditional Love in All Your Relationships

Now that you've worked on harmonizing your relationships, as well as getting rid of any patterns or unresolved issues that can cut off the flow of love and universal energy, you are ready to express oneness in all your relationships. Oneness is a way of seeing everyone's unique connection to the universal energy, a pure connection that you can experience in all your relationships. When you find similarities with everyone you see throughout the day, you bring an unconditional flow of universal energy to everything you do and say.

This is true for all your relationships: your boyfriend, your best friend, your doorman, even the cashier at the supermarket. When you achieve oneness in your relationships, you become a consistent and open channel for psychic energy in every situation, every day. As a conduit for that pure energy, you will more easily find love and happiness reflected back at you wherever you go—not to mention that the constant connection to psychic energy will enable you to become a brighter and more powerful psychic as well.

Creating oneness is about opening to the flow of universal energy when you are dealing with others, and then letting it guide your thoughts and actions. In order to tap into feelings of unconditional love, take a deep breath and fill yourself with universal energy. You may try using a quickie version of one of the techniques from chapter 2. In the In and Up workout you visualized a cylinder at the top of your head opening up to universal energy. In the Grounding workout you used openings at your head and feet as a way to let psychic energy flow through you. And in the Inner Listening exercise you awakened your inner senses of clairaudience, clairvoyance, and clairsentience as a way of connecting to universal energy.

One deep breath, one quickie visualization, and five seconds later you are ready to relate! Since your goal is to express universal energy whenever you come in contact with anyone throughout the day, try this routine before you leave your house, get on the phone, begin a business meeting, or sit down for dinner.

Here are two more quick hints and fun variations on this mini workout that will add oneness to your day. Whenever you come into contact with large numbers of people—as you walk down the street, sit on a train, drive on the highway, or ride an elevator—take a deep breath and send pure universal energy to each person you see. Right before you speak to a friend, family member, or any other special person in your life, take a deep breath and open a psychic connection between the two of you. See, in your mind's eye, how they will respond to you during your conversation.

These quickie techniques have a cumulative effect. You may not notice a difference in your interactions with people the first time you do them, but over time you'll notice that people respond to you with positive openness and their defenses down. It will be easier to get what you want and have a joyful time doing it.

I hope this chapter has helped you learn more about your Self and become more of who you truly are. Whether you're in a relationship now or not, the exercises and information in this chapter have given you a more balanced foundation to build healthy relationships with everyone around you. Putting these steps into action will heal and harmonize your relationship with yourself and others and will help you find fulfilling love in the future.

Now that you know how to do it, there is nothing stopping you from finding your soulmate, getting over lost love, and expressing oneness in every relationship. You'll be much happier; you'll brighten up the lives of everyone you come into contact with; and your popularity will soar!

Set Up a Play Date with Your Mate!

Instead of waiting for a relationship problem to occur before you focus on it, set aside time every week to get psychically in sync with your significant other. During each session, pick any exercise in this book and ask the universe any questions that appeal to both of you. Here are some good ones:

What issues are we working on right now together?

What issues do we have individually that can get in the way of our relationship?

What do we need to know about our relationship now?

What was the significance of [a specific occurrence]?

What are our significant past lives together?

You can even try talking to each other's spirit guides and sharing your journal notes. Making your relationship a conscious one will not only bring you closer to oneness, it will keep your love life in balance and harmony.

chapter six

money, career, and success

▬

When I first started out as a psychic, I had no idea how successful I would become. Reading tarot cards was just something fun I did to make money while I figured out what kind of *real* job I should get. But every time I asked the universe for guidance, for a sign of my destiny, I would get pushed a little farther up the psychic ladder.

The universe told me how to set up promotional materials and where to send them, and that's how I got started doing corporate events and local radio, which eventually led me to doing readings for private clients. A bit farther down the road I asked again, and to my amazement I got the distinct impression that I should write magazine articles. Then it became clear that I should make appearances on television. I am so grateful to my spirit guides and angels for their guidance and patience. Without the help of the universe, I would probably still be lost—and I never would've gotten involved in the media, let alone have written an entire book.

Now that we're on the verge of the new millennium, there are a lot of changes occurring in the world we live in. The old way of being psychic and spiritual was to give up all your earthly possessions, maybe even don a brown or orange robe and shave your head. But today there is nothing wrong with being psychic and spiritual while happily making loads of money—*and* keeping your hair! We are therefore in a unique position to use psychic ability to positively affect careers and money stability. With the universe's help, we can all discover our destined career, increase our income, create our own business, find a great job, make wise investments, even make our current job more enjoyable.

Many clients come to me wanting to change careers, but they don't do it because they are afraid they are going to have to start from scratch at the bottom of the totem pole, low salary and all. Others want to go back to school but are afraid they can't afford tuition, so they stick with the current job they dislike. What is stopping them from enjoying their chosen career and making the money they deserve? Their belief in myths. There are so many work and money horror stories circulating out there; their belief in these stories stops people from following their hearts, their destinies, and their dreams of happiness.

When your actions are based on a belief in stories or myths, you are putting your power and energy into something outside of yourself. As long as you believe these legends are reality, you will never be able to follow your destined career freely. Why are the topics of career and money shrouded in so much myth and mystery? Most of us have learned our work ethics from our parents, and we take these values into our professional lives. Because we see most of the people around us working, we make many assumptions about work and money that are left unexamined. You can use your psychic ability to spot these myths and clear them from your life. Using your inner senses to make decisions about your career and your finances, you can intuit whether you are on a certain path because it is your destiny or because your beliefs and fears are holding you back.

If you break them down, money and career success are currents or paths of energy that stream into and out of our lives. And just like any other current, money and career success ebbs and flows. There are times when we have more activity, and times when we have less. Working with the universe to increase your flow of money and career activity is about finding your ebb and flow and working with that natural energy—to move when the light is green and take a break when the light is red.

Negative money and career myths are just stories of people misunderstanding or going against their natural flow of success. Some people innately understand this flow, while others unknowingly force their natural career movement. Not understanding how to use this flow and

The Ten Best Psychic Career and Money-making Opportunities

One Open a psychic detective agency. Conduct investigations without ever leaving the office!

Two Breed psychic chickens. They won't have to cross the road to get to the other side.

Three Manufacture Psychic Elmo dolls. Squeeze their tummies, and they make scandalous predictions about the Cookie Monster.

Four How about a psychic window-washer? No need for scaffolding when you can levitate.

Five Play "Psychic Jeopardy." Contestants aren't given the answers or the questions. In fact, the host doesn't even say a word; he just *thinks* a lot.

Six Rent yourself out as a human fax machine. Hey, if you can send and receive thoughts, why not faxes?

Seven Become a telekinetic basketball player. There is no height requirement, just the ability to use mind over matter.

Eight Be the first psychic sportscaster. Call the game with your eyes closed.

Nine Try your hand as the universe's radio transmitter. You're picking up the signal anyway, you might as well pass it along!

Ten Become the sixth Spice Girl, Psychic Spice.

not paying attention to intuition can wreak havoc on your career. Some people create businesses when it is the perfect time for expansion and they become successful overnight, while others can't seem to get a new job no matter how hard they try. By listening to your inner senses, you will be able to make career and money decisions based on your intuition and your psychic timing. Psychic timing is the universe's timing. Your internal psychic clock tells you the right time to move ahead and the right time to lie low.

Some business analysts might say, "Why do you need your intuition, when you have access to so many expert speakers, books, and magazines on career and money?" In this day and age, there are no rules to doing business anymore. The impossible is coming true all the time. No one is dictating the up and down numbers of the stock market, interest rates, and employment opportunities. The best source for success is your internal senses. Use them and you cannot go wrong.

This chapter is dedicated to understanding the psychic side of moneymaking and career success, and to enabling you to connect with your destiny and manifest that unique side of you through a successful balance of creativity and discipline. The exercises that follow will show you how to make money and career decisions based on intuitive knowledge and how to be comfortable following decisions made from the heart, not just from the mind. Then you will be able to find the perfect career, enjoy your job, make a comfortable amount of money, and start and grow your own business with reduced risk of anxiety, stress, or financial loss.

Finding Your Perfect Career

Do you absolutely love your job, or are you feeling stuck in a deadend career? Maybe you enjoy your career, but you feel that there are more and bigger things for you out there. Even if you are only mildly dissatisfied, there is no reason to go to the same job every day if it is in any way limiting your sense of happiness and well-being. If you are disappointed with your job or think you might enjoy a different career, it's time to take a closer look at your destiny, or life path, to see if it needs some realignment.

Everybody has a destiny, a unique path that is fulfilling and successful. This is the path that is best suited for you to learn your lessons and grow as a soul. Everyone who is happy within his career is following his life path, whether he is aware of it or not. Most people who are unhappy either don't know their path or are afraid to take the necessary steps to follow it. In this chapter I'll show you a simple exercise that will help you uncover your path as well as the steps you need to take to get on that road and ensure your success. Since your destiny is a given, once it's found, there will be no stopping you.

Even though your life path is the perfect path for you, it is usually intertwined with some lessons along the way, and part of understanding your destiny is understanding those lessons. If your destiny is to be an artist and you are afraid of rejection, then you will never allow yourself to follow your life path unless you take on the lessons of rejection. You may know your path, but if something stops you from taking action, you will not be able to complete your destiny. When you look at the total picture—career destiny and life lessons—you can clearly see the rewards of all of your actions. The artist's path becomes easy to follow when you know that on the other side of that rejection letter is a destiny that includes a good news phone call from an art gallery.

When you know your right path and you take action, you are guaranteed success, because this is your destiny, but it is important to remember that you are working with the universe to affect your destiny. Working with the flow of your success means working with the greater timing of the universe. When you ask the universe for the actions to take in order to follow your life path, you also want to ask for the appropriate timing for these actions. The same action would bring you success whenever you acted on it, but it would be most effective when coupled with the right timing. For example, if you learn that your path as an artist involves taking a loan and opening your own studio; the universe may also tell you to wait a few months because interest rates will go down. The best way for you to find success is to take other actions in the meantime—like filing all the correct legal documents—until the time arrives when it will be most beneficial for you to take out a loan.

Our life path changes every few years as we learn and grow, so it is important to check in with the universe at the first sign of discontent so that you can discover any changes in your life path as they occur. That will maximize the flow of energy in your life and thereby maximize your success.

The Discover Your Career Destiny exercise that follows is made up of three steps:

1. *Discovering your destiny along with the lessons on your life path*
2. *Discovering the necessary steps to get you on track and keep you there, as well as the perfect timing for these steps*
3. *Putting those steps into action*

Steps 1 and 2 will not work without step 3. Since actions are what get you closer to the destiny you've uncovered, after you do this exercise, you *must* apply for that new job, look into job skills training, or open your new business. It'll work out fine, with the universe on your side.

Psychic Workout
Discover Your Career Destiny

Begin by taking out your notebook and writing down some appropriate questions. Here are some good ones:

What do I need to know about my current job?
What career path or destiny am I supposed to be on right now?
What has changed about my life path recently?
What lessons am I learning on my path right now?
What fears do I have about my destiny?
What beliefs do I have about my career destiny?

To receive the answers to your questions, choose one of the following information-gathering exercises in chapter 4:

Communicating with the Universe
Magnetizing Information
Finding Your Psychic Solution

Because the last two questions are related to fears and beliefs, you may also use the Fears and Beliefs workout (chapter 3) to receive the answers to your questions.

Once you understand your destined career path and the lessons you are learning along the way, use an information-gathering exercise to ask the universe for the actions you can take to fulfill that path.

What can I best do to follow this path?
What is the best timing for these actions?
What can I best do to learn my life path's lessons?
What can I do to effectively release any negative fears or beliefs?

Then take the appropriate actions every day to bring you closer to that path.

Ten Seconds to a Yes or a No Answer!

Have you ever had the experience of trying to order food for the company picnic and wondering if you should make ninety-five percent of the staff happy with grilled chicken at the expense of the boss's vegetarian secretary? When buying your mom a sweater for her birthday, have you ever felt paralyzed with indecision over choosing between the red flowers or the blue snowflakes? If you feel constantly bothered by difficult decisions, here's the solution. No more wishy-washy uncertainty for you! With the help of the universe, you can get a concrete yes or no answer to any question in a matter of seconds. This may seem a bit far out, but I assure you, it works like a charm.

Or should I say *coin?* Here's what you do. Whenever you want a quickie answer, take a coin in your hand. Close your eyes and awaken your inner senses. Ask, "What side of this coin is yes?" Then flip the coin and see which end is up. That is the yes side of the coin, according to the universe. Now, flip the coin again while asking a question in a yes-or-no fashion. *Should I order pizza for tomorrow's big meeting? If I send my résumé today, will the boss get it before the weekend? Will Dad like this pair of gloves better than that one?*

After you have used this psychic trick a few times, you may begin to notice a pattern as you ask the preliminary question, "What side of the coin is yes?" Once you receive the same answer consistently to that question, know that in your universe, tails tends to always mean yes. You can skip that step and go straight to your question.

Creating and Growing the Perfect Business

More and more people are running their own businesses these days: creating freelance services to bring in extra cash, joining with family members to create a home-owned company, even choosing consulting and flextime work over a nine-to-five grind. If you are looking to make additional income, or if you already have a business up and running, psychic energy can help you strengthen your ideas and put them into action, bringing your business prosperity and growth.

There are many risks involved when you start and run your own business, and you may have many questions. Is the product you are thinking of selling a quality product? Is your service competitive in the marketplace? Are you getting enough customers to create growth? Is this a good opportunity, or are you going to end up closing up shop after losing a fortune? Without psychic energy, answering these questions would rely on a lot of guesswork. You can take the guesswork out by working with universal energy.

Since psychic ability helps you see your unique destiny and your professional talents and future rewards, the idea of using it to facilitate the creation of your own business seems perfectly natural. Using a combination of regular psychic exercises and practical actions, you can discover the best actions to take to achieve your goals, take those actions, and check in regularly with the universe to ensure that each progression is in harmony with the "big picture" of your destiny. This process can alleviate much of the anxiety that comes with starting and running a successful business, helping you more easily make decisions that affect others. You'll feel safer following your ideas, and you'll feel more comfortable taking financial risks.

Psychic Workout
Start Your Own Business with Universal Assurance

Begin by taking out your notebook and writing a few appropriate business questions. Here are a few examples:

What would be the perfect business for me?
What business would I find fun and successful?
How can I make my current business more prosperous?
How can I best create this business?
What is the next step/steps I should take to ensure my success?

Choose any one of the following information-gathering exercises from chapter 4 and use it to learn the answers to these questions.

Communicating with the Universe
Magnetizing Information
Finding Your Psychic Solution

Once you have received the answers to your questions, it's time to formulate the best plan of action. Using the answers you just received, map out a plan of steps to take to ensure your success.

While you formulate your plan of action, you may also come up with a few additional questions about this plan. Maybe you know that your next step is to make a business proposal, but you're not sure if the timing is correct. Using an information-gathering exercise, ask the appropriate questions that will clarify everything for you.

Once you know the steps to take and have clarified all the loose ends, begin to take those steps. Whenever you have progressed to a new action—whether it is every few days or few weeks—remember to check in with the universe again by revisiting this exercise. Recalculate your plan and ask any necessary questions about your next steps.

AT A GLANCE

Start Your Own Business with Universal Assurance

Step One Write appropriate business-related questions in your notebook.

Step Two Use one of the information-gathering exercises from chapter 4 to learn the answers to these questions.

Step Three Using the answers you received, formulate the best plan of action to ensure your success.

Step Four Get back into a meditative state to receive clarification if necessary.

Step Five Take those steps.

Step Six Whenever you have progressed to a new action, check in with the universe again and ask appropriate questions.

Nail a Job Interview in Advance

Nervous about a job interview? It's easy to use your psychic connection to make a power connection with your interviewer and instantly provide just the answer he or she wants to hear.

You can do this by setting up a special psychic session before your interview. Depending on how important the interview is to you and how much free time you have, you may want to have a five-minute session every day for a couple of days until the big date. During each session, take out your résumé and any information you have about the prospective company. This information will help you focus on exactly what you wish to achieve. It may be the classified ad you answered, an advertisement you've seen in a magazine, or the business card of a friend who already works there.

Create your sacred space, take a few deep breaths, and get into a meditative state. Visualize your upcoming interview from start to finish. See the interviewer enjoying you from the first handshake to the last goodbyes. Hear all his or her questions and your answers. See the energy flowing freely as you speak honestly and gracefully. Affirm that you are the best person for the job—that you are fabulous and that this company is completely excited as they hire you on the spot. Before your interview, do a quickie version of the Magnetizing Your Goals exercise (chapter 4). Focus on getting the job. Attract to yourself all the empowering feelings that go along with doing a great job and fulfilling your destiny.

Go to the interview while you are in that magnetic state. As you travel there, send some pure energy to the interviewer, put a protective shield around yourself, and Put an Angel on Your Shoulder (page 211). You will be ready to psychically attract that job, and you will have your best interview ever!

Making Your Job More Enjoyable

Perhaps you are confident that you are in your destined career, but you would like your current employment to be a little more interesting. Do you enjoy your job but dislike your boss? Maybe you would like to work fewer hours, or perhaps you wish you could be more confident when you give group presentations. If you have small complaints like these, there is no need to take a drastic action such as looking for a new job when a minor adjustment to your current work experience can make all the difference in the world.

We all have areas of our work we dislike, but this doesn't mean we are ready to give up the job altogether. Rather than accepting unresolved issues as part of the job, or continually working on releasing negative feelings that these problems can bring about, you can ask for the universe's assistance to fix the parts of your job you dislike.

Don't worry about identifying *everything* about your job that you have an aversion to; the following exercise will enable you to transcend issues without controlling every last detail. It contains a short statement and visualization designed to be repeated several times in the same session. As you do this, amazing things will begin to happen. Your boss will take a vacation and come back a new (and better!) person. You will be offered a nice raise. Your hours will shorten. Minor changes will occur that make your job easier and more fulfilling. You may even see *more* positive changes than you thought you wanted!

Psychic Workout
Change Your Job Without Changing Your Job

Begin by closing your eyes and creating a ball of light three or four feet above you and in front of you, so that you can visualize it comfortably in your mind's eye without discomfort to your neck. This is the energy of the universe: your spirit guides, angels, Higher Self, or God.

Take a few deep breaths, and pull pure universal energy from the ball. Visually send it down through your body, as you repeat a positive statement several times. Because of the variety of problems that can occur within any job, you can either write your own personal statement or use this one:

Dear Spirit, I give you my job (as well as any related unresolved issue). Fix it, heal it, and return it to me whole. Thank you.

*As you repeat the statement, visualize yourself handing your job and
all its issues to the ball of light. Let the universe fix the problems and hand
it back to you. Repeat this for one to two minutes, several times a day.*

*You can also add Affirmations and Visualizations (chapter 3) mini
sessions to your day. Try affirmations such as* Every aspect of my job is
fabulous. My boss adores me. *Visualize images of yourself enjoying the
particular aspect of your work that you currently dislike. Feel yourself enjoying these aspects of your work as if they are occurring today. When you
affirm and visualize changes as though they're already occurring, your
everyday reality changes to match your intentions.*

Increasing Your Money Flow

Do you make a decent living, yet find that you are struggling to make
ends meet every month? Are you comfortable with your take-home
salary but wanting to increase your income for future investments? No
matter what your money situation is—whether you are flat broke,
rolling in dough, or somewhere in between—you can work with psychic energy to increase your money flow, have more cash left over after paying your bills, and ensure that you have more than enough
money to fulfill your happiness and the happiness of others.

There are three parts to this exercise:

*1. Examining any limitations that may stop you from increasing your
flow of money*
2. Releasing any negative beliefs you may hold about earning money
3. Using the universal energy to increase money in your life

Your financial status is directly related to the beliefs you hold about money, as well as the life lessons you are currently learning. If you are unhappy with your money flow, it may be due to the presence of negative or limiting beliefs about money floating around in your belief system. You will not be able to increase your money flow unless you reevaluate those beliefs and release any negativity that may be getting in your way.

Changing your beliefs will increase your money flow, but your beliefs don't make up your entire daily experiences with money; you must also take into consideration the lessons you are currently dealing with. If you are supposed to be learning to truly appreciate yourself deep to the core of your soul, you may find that your cash flow is drying up. By making it harder for you to have distractions such as pedicures, sporting equipment, and new electronic toys, the universe ensures that the only thing you are left to focus on is You.

We've already looked into the lessons that are intertwined with your career destiny in the first exercise in this chapter. In order to understand your lessons with money, in the next exercise you are going to look into your beliefs and fears as they directly relate to money. Career lessons and money lessons can be very different. For example, your career lessons may involve dealing with your fears of success, while your money lessons may involve getting rid of a belief of not having enough. So along with looking for any negative or limiting beliefs and fears that you may have, the question you will be focusing on in this next exercise is: *What lessons do I need to learn or am I currently learning about money?* By identifying all the sources that may be causing you to have discomfort with your flow of money—both beliefs and lessons—you will then be free to use the power of the universal energy to create all sorts of extra money in your life.

Increasing your money flow is easy once your life is clear of these beliefs, fears, and lessons. You can work on increasing your money from traditional sources, such as getting a raise, and I'll show you a few mini exercises to bring money in from all sorts of other sources. You can increase your annual tax refund, win the lottery, even find money stuck in the toe of an old pair of shoes. The trick to receiving money with the help of the universe is to think broadly; you will only receive money from odd sources if you believe in all the possibilities. Once you unlimit your mind and visualize all the ways money can come to you, you'll find it streaming in from all over the place.

One last thing. When I say that the universe can help you increase your money flow, I don't just mean that money will start falling into your wallet (although it may!). I also mean that the universe can help you painlessly reduce your expenses in ways you may not even notice until you suddenly notice a surplus in your disposable income. For example, as you do these exercises, you may find that you win a free month of groceries, the phone company lowers your monthly charges, or you discover great coupons for half-price dry cleaning.

Psychic Workout
Multiply Your Money

The first step toward increasing your money is to clarify your beliefs about it. Begin by taking out your notebook and writing appropriate questions. Here are some good ones:

What are my beliefs about money?
What are my fears about money?
What is my relationship with money?

Use the Fears and Beliefs exercise (chapter 3) to learn the answers to your questions. These answers should reveal any negative or limiting beliefs you have that may be getting in the way of creating a good money flow in your life. Next, work on releasing any negativity you may have found by creating a list of positive Affirmations and Visualizations (chapter 3) and repeating them during a few psychic sessions. Continue to follow the

Fears and Beliefs workout by creating a corresponding list of positive be-liefs to replace the negative beliefs.

Once you have freed yourself of any negative thoughts, you are ready to address any money lessons you are learning and any actions you can take to get over those issues, as well as any actions you can take to increase your money flow. Using an information-gathering exercise, ask yourself the following questions:

What lessons am I learning about money?
How do these destined lessons affect my money situation?
How can I best learn these lessons?
What can I do to increase my flow of money?

Once you have the answers to these questions, take the necessary actions you uncovered. You can also use some quickie mini sessions along with these actions to increase your money intake. Magnetizing Your Goals (chapter 4) is the perfect workout to magnetize more money into your life. During full sessions or mini sessions, awaken your magnetic qualities and envision all the different ways you can receive money. I love doing this exercise to attract money. I visualize myself attracting money as if my skin is glue: money coming from all sources, all directions, sticking to me like corn flakes to honey!

Another good exercise you can do to raise your money intake is the Be-coming Comfortable with your Destiny workout (chapter 3). As you cre-ate the perfect You in the pod, see yourself holding so many stacks of twenty-dollar bills that you can hardly carry anything else. Envision your-self with loads of money in your checking account, your savings account, your stock portfolio, your wallet, and any other place you want to keep a stash. As you pull the pod around you, living the perfect You, feel yourself with all of that money; see yourself inspired as you spend it to further your happiness and the happiness of others.

Do these exercises for three to four minutes, three times a day. You should see your income increase immediately.

Multiply Your Money

Step One Take out your notebook and write appropriate questions concerning your beliefs about money.

Step Two Use the Fears and Beliefs workout to receive your answers to these questions and create a list of positive beliefs about money.

Step Three Release any negativity you may have found by creating a list of Affirmations and Visualizations.

Step Four Get back into a meditative state and ask yourself questions to discover any money lessons you may be learning. Seek to uncover actions you can take to get over those issues, and any actions you can take to increase your money flow.

Step Five Take those actions, with or without any of the mini session exercises just suggested.

Getting out of Debt and into Prosperity

Whenever I watch a TV show about finances, invariably the topic turns to the debt weighing down most American households. The last time I looked, each and every family in this country carries a personal debt in the neighborhood of $7,000 and rising. It seems everyone's affected in some way: credit card bills, department store charges, student loans, car payments. If you are one of the lucky few these days who carries no debt, good for you. If you're like the rest of us average Joes, there are things you can do—other than cut up your credit cards and declare bankruptcy—to get control of the problem and eliminate debt from your life altogether.

I know what you're thinking. (I am a psychic, after all!) *If I have debt, why can't I just get rid of it by increasing my income using the Mul-*

Mass Mailing Your Résumé or Business Flyer?
Use Psychic Energy and Be Sure to Get a Response!

When you are looking for a new job, you may mail your résumé cold to twenty-five different companies and give it to scores of headhunters and employment agencies. Similarly, when you are expanding or starting your own business, you may send out mailings to hundreds of local customers who have never heard of you before. Take heart—you don't have to feel that all this effort is a big shot in the dark. By using the power of universal energy, you can make sure your mailing stands out from the pack.

Before you do any kind of mass mailing or cold calling, schedule a special psychic session to infuse your résumés or flyers with pure energy from the universe. Create your sacred space, then pick up one of your résumés or flyers and close your eyes. Open your connection to the universe at the top of your head and pull down the universal energy. Send it through your body and fingers right into the paper. At the same time, visualize your résumé reaching its destination and landing at the *top* of the recipient's pile of incoming mail. See the recipient reading it and being impressed. Visualize the company calling you. This should take fifteen to twenty seconds. As you finish with each résumé or flyer, go on to another until you've infused all of the résumés in your pile.

Items inoculated with universal energy operate in strange ways. Clients have often reported that my business card kept popping up in the front of their wallets for weeks until they called me; or the audiotape of their last session with me kept popping off their shelf and onto the middle of the floor. If this technique works for cassette tapes, why not use it to get more interviews and increase sales?

tiply Your Money workout in the last section? You can. But if you're in debt, the actual money owed is only one of two different problems at work in your life. To effectively increase your prosperity and get rid of your debt, you not only have to increase your money flow but also must deal with any underlying negative issues that may be the real source of your debts.

These issues may involve limiting beliefs you are holding onto about money or fears of success that are keeping you from experiencing your full money potential. Debt is a symptom of deeper unlearned lessons as well. If you need to learn self-love but feel you are too unworthy to love yourself, and do not address that issue, you may find that you are always broke. You will never allow yourself to enjoy anything you don't feel you deserve; and how can you be in the position to enjoy anything if you can't afford it? Pinpointing the cause of your debt will enable you to take the proper steps to eliminate that debt from your life. Then you are free to work on raising your level of comfort when it comes to money and increasing the money in your life.

The next exercise is geared toward getting to the issues behind your debt: the unresolved problems, fears, and beliefs that may be keeping you in a place of financial discomfort and debt. As soon as you identify the issues behind your debts, you will see your situation change. Then, as you release the beliefs, fears, and issues attached to your debt, you will not only be free of your debt, you will also see your flow of money increase to a comfortable amount.

Psychic Workout
Erasing Debt from Your Life

The first step toward releasing your debt is to clarify your beliefs about it. Begin by taking out your notebook and writing down a few questions:

What are my beliefs about debt?
What are my fears about debt?

Use the Fears and Beliefs workout to receive the answers to your questions. These answers should reveal any limiting or negative beliefs that may be keeping you tied to your debt. Next, work on releasing any negative or limiting beliefs and fears you may have found by creating a list of affirmations and visualizations. Continue to follow the Fears and Beliefs exercise by creating a list of positive beliefs to replace any negative or limiting ones.

As you begin to release your negative beliefs and fears about your debt, go on to the next step: addressing the underlying causes of your debt and discovering any actions you can take to rid yourself of the debt as well as the issues that caused it. To do that, choose any of the information-gathering exercises in chapter 4 and ask yourself some well-thought-out questions. Here are some good ones:

Why do I have debt in my life?
What is the issue(s) behind my debt?
What can I do to erase this debt from my life?
What can I do to release this issue from my life?

Once you have the answers to these questions, take the necessary steps you uncovered. Continue to do your affirmations and visualizations as well as study your new set of beliefs. After a few weeks of doing this, you should be able to see your debt dwindling as you get control of deeper unresolved issues in your life.

Once you have released the underlying issues, you are free to do exercises to increase the flow of money in your life. Try Magnetizing Your Goals (chapter 4). Awaken your magnetic qualities and envision all the different ways you can receive money. Do Becoming Comfortable with Your Destiny (chapter 3) as well. As you create the perfect You in the pod, see yourself with tons of money in as many ways as you can. As you pull the pod around you, living the perfect You, feel yourself with all of that money as if it is your reality right now.

AT A GLANCE
Erasing Debt from Your life

Step One Write questions about your debts and bills in your notebook.

Step Two Use the Fears and Beliefs workout to receive your answers to these questions.

Step Three Release any negativity you may have found by creating a list of affirmations and visualizations as well as a list of positive beliefs.

Step Four Using any of the information-gathering-exercises from chapter 4, ask yourself appropriate questions about your debt and its underlying issues. Seek to uncover any actions you can take to work through these issues.

Step Five After your underlying issues are released, increase the flow of money in your life by using the Magnetizing Your Goals and Becoming Comfortable with Your Destiny exercises.

Making Psychic Investments

Whether you are investing to buy a house or making sure you have enough money for your child's college education or your own retirement, you need to be wise about your choices today to make the most of your money tomorrow. Usually people think of investing as a purely logical speculation, a rational matter of reading the *Wall Street Journal* and financial magazines to get information on hot stocks and solid properties. Not so. You can make solid investments using information you receive during your psychic sessions. You will be able to pick hot stocks, know what investments to stay away from, and know when to sell your investments to bring the highest returns. Given the volatility of the financial market, you can use your psychic ability—in addition to advice from the experts—to be doubly sure that your investments will be solid moneymakers.

This is not that difficult, and it takes no more time than doing traditional research. It just involves asking the right questions and earmarking a few psychic sessions. It is crucial that you have all the information necessary to make an investment wisely before you act with intention. Maybe your broker has recommended that you invest in a new computer company. He gives you the company's history and financial records as well as information about the product they are developing. Before you go ahead and invest, you ask the universe some well-thought-out questions: Will this product have problems in development? How long will it take for this product to get to the marketplace? When this product gets on the market, how well will it sell? Will strong sales drive the stock prices up? No matter how good the analysts are, these are questions they cannot definitely answer. By receiving this information psychically before you invest, you will be able to make more thoroughly informed decisions.

Psychic information works hand in hand with expert advice. You can only learn a certain amount from hard research, so use your psychic ability and you will leave nothing to chance. You can fill in the blanks left by market analysis as well as confirm future trends before they happen.

While you can use psychic energy to get any answer to any question about any investment, there is a catch. You will only be able to use psychic energy to invest in something that is not only for your good but for the greater good of all things. For example, if you are considering investing in a fur company or a conglomerate whose wastes are poisoning the environment, there is no way you'll be able to use your psychic ability to make money from these stocks. When you ask questions about one of these stocks, you may not receive the detailed responses you need to effectively make good decisions. Or you may receive information about the companies' practices that may persuade you not to invest in them after all.

When you get investment ideas and information from your psychic sessions, you will feel more comfortable knowing that your financial research is backed up by your inner senses and the power and insight of the universe. You will be less worried about daily ups and downs, and more assured of the end results of an investment. With the universe on your side, you'll never have to worry about your investment choices again!

Psychic Workout
Investing the Psychic Way

Make a list of investments that you are interested in receiving more information about. They can be investments that you currently hold or investments you are thinking about making. Write the name of the first investment in your notebook along with some appropriate questions about it. Here are a few good ones:

Is this a good investment for me?
Is this a good long-term or short-term investment?
If I buy this, when is the best time to sell it?
What do I need to know about this investment?
Will I be happy with this investment?

Pick one of the information-gathering exercises from chapter 4 to learn the answers to these questions. When you are finished with the first investment, write the next one from your original list in your notebook, and ask the same questions about it.

On the basis of this information, make your investment strategy a combination of logic and intuition that draws on both solid financial research and the wisdom of the universe. Don't be afraid to discount the experts if your information is contradictory. If you want to double-check the answers you've received psychically before putting any money into an investment, write out a list of the investments you're questioning and do the Ten Seconds to a Yes or a No exercise on page 150. Ask the same yes or no ques-

tion for each of the investments: Is this a good investment for me? *Write down all the answers.*

After rereading all your answers, you may possibly come up with a few more clarifying questions. Let's say the universe told you that you will be relatively happy with several of your investments. Understandably, you want to know what, if any, are the weaknesses of these investments. Don't hesitate to use one of the information-gathering exercises to get clarification of your previous answers. Formulate some appropriate questions, get back into a meditative state, and receive the information you need to make your investments wisely.

Plan Your Business Meeting with Universal Energy

With meetings and conferences, as with job interviews, chances are that no matter how much you prepare, some aspects of your plan may fall out of your control. You may find that a scheduling conflict has put a hitch in your plans. Your conference call may go awry. If you use psychic energy as a planning tool, however, you may never again have to worry about the outcome of a meeting.

Two days before your meeting, schedule a psychic session to do some affirmation and visualization work. Begin your session as you normally would, by creating your sacred space and getting into a meditative state. Begin to visualize your meeting. Verbally describe the perfect meeting as you flow through the proposed agenda. Affirm that your meeting will be magical; that all parties will agree on all its aspects.

Do this at least two times before your meeting. Make sure you define which meeting you are trying to affect, or you may find the universe helping you with some other meeting sometime in the future.

Just before the actual meeting takes place, do a quickie thirty-second session. Visualize the meeting going smoothly, and affirm that it will unfold exactly as you wish. Send pure universal energy to everyone involved, awaken your magnetic qualities, and walk in the door with confidence. You'll see all the parties coming together in harmony as your meeting progresses beautifully.

One final point. Now that you know how to discover your career destiny, and now that you have as much money as you need coming in, you can drop all your worries about success and financial stability. But remember, money and success are flowing energy currents—currents that change throughout your life. To stay in control of your destiny, you need to remember to periodically check in with the universe and stay in touch with the direction and the velocity of that flow of energy. A little psychic homework goes a long way toward giving you the knowledge and understanding of your life path that you need to ride the wave to career and financial success.

chapter seven

health and physical appearance

━━━

A few years ago I was very busy with my work, spending most of my time during the week doing private consultations. If I wasn't shuffling tarot cards, I was writing—magazine articles, sitcom scripts, the proposal for this book. Between shuffling cards for hours on end and using the mouse on my computer, my right wrist and arm began to ache terribly. I spent a lot of time with it wrapped in an Ace bandage until one night when a group of spirit guides woke me up to tell me something.

I picked up the notebook that I keep in bed, and immediately began to take dictation. My wrist began to ache, and I was so annoyed that I telepathically let them have it. "You want me to write this down, fine. I'll write everything down, and you can keep using me as a conduit to reach others, but I don't want this pain anymore. So if you want me to continue writing for you, take this pain away." Boom! Immediately it was gone. I was mesmerized. I spent half the night shaking my wrist to make sure the pain wasn't coming back. Nearly two years later, it's still gone!

This is not one isolated incidence of spontaneous healing. With the right know-how, you too can get rid of aches and pains, heal illness, and restore balanced energy and health to any part of your body using the power of your body-mind-soul connection.

The Ten Best Ways to Spot Another Psychic Person

One Go into a crowded room and think, "Fire!" Without a doubt, those who run out are psychic, too.

Two When you go to shake a person's hand, he reads your palm instead.

Three If a gypsy has tarot cards and she's *not* playing five-card stud, you know she must be for real.

Four You spot a guy in front of the lottery machine, sitting in a lotus position with magnets taped to his head. You'll know he's psychically attempting to extract the day's numbers.

Five If you see a woman walking backward down the sidewalk without stepping on any cracks, you know she's superstitious *and* psychic.

Six You can spot two psychic friends if their conversations consist of staring at each other and saying, "I know," "I know."

Seven You dial information looking for the phone number of the hottest restaurant in town, and the operator picks up and says, "It's 555-8594. You're a psychic. Next time, get it yourself."

Eight If you spot a guy driving around asking a magic 8-ball for directions, he's either desperately lost or psychic.

Nine If you're in Las Vegas and you see a band of people levitating in the middle of the slot machines with their eyes closed, chanting, "Om, show me the money!" pay attention to where they land; they're bound to make a lot of money.

Ten You enter an abandoned house and you spot mice jumping around on a Ouija board, and they're spelling your name. Listen up, 'cause they're psychic.

We all want to be as healthy as we can be, and this chapter will help you maximize your health. If you already feel good, then you can feel better. You will learn to maximize your energy, get a more restful sleep, and create a perfect eating plan to stay fit. If you suffer from a health problem, you will learn how to use psychic energy to heal aches and pains; relieve chronic illnesses like asthma and arthritis; and address the underlying causes of these illnesses.

Being maximally healthy means having balanced energy. Health problems often begin as an imbalance in the connection between your body, mind, and soul. When you are stressed for any length of time without giving yourself a chance to recover, chances are the stress will release itself in your body, giving you a cold, back pain, a migraine, or any number of other problems. That is why balancing energy is so important. I will show you how to rebalance your energy during your psychic sessions on a regular basis; then you will work on any imbalance before it becomes physical, enabling you to maintain good health and vitality.

You may be in great health, but even the healthiest person still gets occasional headaches, sore muscles, and broken bones. When you have a minor ache or pain, you can use psychic energy to alleviate the symptoms as well as heal broken bones and sore muscles. The information-gathering exercises in chapter 4 will help you analyze the underlying issues behind your heath problems. Becoming Comfortable with Your Destiny will help you envision and realize yourself in perfect health, and Magnetizing Your Goals will magnetize good health to you.

I know what you're thinking: *If optimum health is so natural and self-healing is so easy, why doesn't everybody know about this?* Most of us were brought up to believe in conventional medicine and nothing more. Being able to heal our own bodies goes against everything we are taught by society. And, as you already know from earlier chapters, you only get what you believe in. If your only belief reference is to conventional medicine, you'll never believe in your power to heal yourself.

Let's examine conventional limiting health beliefs for a moment. You are diagnosed with a minor problem, and the doctor tells you all the different ways you can live with it. You can take medicine, do a certain kind of therapy, or avoid overusing that part of your body. Unconsciously, you take stock of the pain, if it is minor, and on an unconscious level, you decide to live with it. *Oh, it's just my nervous stomach acting up again—I'll take an antacid.* When you do that, what you are really doing is accepting the problem—saying to the universe, "I can deal with this."

You may have bad knees from playing high school football, a bad back because it runs in your family, an irregular heartbeat, or an allergy to dust. Under conventional Western medicine, you naturally accept these problems as reality. We accept illnesses all the time without thinking twice; this is an action based on the belief that it is perfectly normal to have some health problems. When we accept aches, pains, or illness, we don't take appropriate actions to get to the bottom of the imbalance and erase the problem from our lives. But when we believe in our ability to heal and work with the universal energy to release any issues that separate us from our good health, we can bring our bodies back to their natural healthy state.

You may find comfort in traditional medicine, and that's perfectly fine. I am not saying don't go to doctors; I go to doctors when it's necessary. You do not have to give up your belief in doctors to believe in your body's natural healthy state. When you do any of the recommended health exercises in this chapter, what you are really doing is enabling yourself to look deeper into the condition of your health and to use the universal energy to reaffirm and restore your optimum health.

This chapter isn't just about health, it's about all things physical. After we work on our insides, we are going to concentrate on our outsides: working on whatever aspect of our physical body that we desire to change. You can lose or gain weight, change the shape of your butt, even reduce wrinkles. A good strong connection to psychic energy can enhance all areas of your life, not just the ones deemed "spiritual."

Psychic energy is an illusion-buster. It can do all sorts of supposedly impossible things. You may have a health problem or a body image issue that everyone says will never go away, but if you don't accept it in your life, the universe won't either. By inviting the universal energy to work with you, you can create miracles with your body, mind, and soul. The bottom line: It doesn't matter what anyone thinks of your body or health problems, it's what you think and what you do that determine your physical well-being.

Rebalance Your Energy and Stay Healthy

Because many of our health issues come from an energy imbalance within our bodies, it is very important that we rebalance our energy on a regular basis whether or not we feel sick. We do this often without even knowing it. Do you close your eyes at work and take a catnap in the afternoon? Or sleep for ten hours at night after an especially busy day? This is your body's way of telling you it needs to restore its energy.

The following exercise, an expansion of the Relaxing with the Universe workout from chapter 1, helps you consciously restore your energy, enabling you to maintain balanced health. It not only works to rebalance your energy to keep you healthy; it will also help you restore energy during an illness. Working with the universal energy when you are sick will aid your body in fighting off infection and get rid of any stored-up negative energy.

During this exercise, you're going to work with the experts: your angels and spirit guides. There are angels for everything, including healing, and I will provide you with a properly worded invitation you can use to call on them. You may feel them, you may not feel them, it doesn't matter. Either way they will be there assisting you.

I know there are a lot of detailed instructions in the following exercise. Don't get caught up in doing all the steps exactly as they are written, or you may end up choking off the flow of universal energy. Feel free to play it by ear a bit. The more you do this, the more second-nature the exercise becomes. The most important part is having an open and continuous flow of pure universal energy to heal and rebalance your body.

Psychic Workout
Rebalance Your Energy, Restore Your Health

Begin by creating your sacred space and lying in a comfortable position. Get into a basic meditative state. As you breathe deeply, surround yourself with a womb of love and light large enough to cradle your whole body comfortably. Visually extend an umbilical cord from that womb about five feet out into the universe. On the other end of the cord are your angels and spirit guides.

Imagine pulling the universal energy through the cord and into each part of your body: your feet, ankles, calves, knees, pelvis, hips, stomach, ribs, chest, down through your arms, to your elbows, hands, and fingers; back to your shoulders, neck, jaw, face, and head.

When you are comfortable and relaxed, you are ready to restore the energy to the different parts of your body. First, you must release any negative energy residue that has left stress in your body. To do that, call in the experts: the angels and archangels in charge of healing. Repeat the following statement:

All the healing angels and archangels, please assist me in releasing any energy in my body that is not for my greatest good. As I concentrate on individual parts of my body, work with me to discharge any unhealthy or destructive energy.

With your universal helpers, scan your body, going through each part, one by one. Focus on releasing and draining all the negative energy that you come across. Move through your feet, ankles, calves, knees, pelvis, hips, stomach, ribs, chest, down through your arms, to your elbows, hands, and fingers. Go back to your shoulders, neck, jaw, face, and head. Drain the negative energy completely from one area before moving on to the next. This should be easy, because you won't find negative energy everywhere; you'll probably find it in only three to six areas of your body. The rest will be clear.

Now that your body is balanced and neutralized, call on your angels and guides one more time to work with you to infuse those weak spots you found with pure white light from the universe.

Guides and Angels, help me to restore the vital energy within my body, infusing each depleted area with pure universal energy, and restoring the balance and harmony within my body, mind, and soul.

With the assistance of your guides, pull the pure universal energy through your umbilical cord and send it to each part of your body. End your session by wrapping a golden cocoon of protection around you. Close your sacred space and write in your journal.

AT A GLANCE
Rebalance Your Energy, Restore Your Health

Step One Create your sacred space and get into a basic meditative state.

Step Two As you breathe deeply, surround yourself with a womb of love and light large enough to cradle your whole body comfortably. Visually extend an umbilical cord from that womb about five feet out into the universe.

Step Three Pull the universal energy through the cord into each part of your body.

Step Four Call all the angels and archangels in charge of healing. Ask them to help you to discharge any unhealthy energy.

Step Five Scan your body, going through each area, focusing on releasing and draining any negative energy that you come across.

Step Six Now that your body is balanced and neutralized, call on your angels and guides to work with you to restore all the weak spots.

Step Seven Pull the pure universal energy through your umbilical cord and send it to each part of your body, focusing on restoring the energy there.

Step Eight End your session by wrapping a spun-gold cocoon of protection around yourself. Close your sacred space and write in your journal.

Getting a Spiritually Sound Sleep

Being healthy not only means enjoying productive days. Having healthy, balanced energy means getting a good night's sleep as well. Sleep time is a time when we all naturally recharge. Using the universal energy as you fall asleep will help you maximize your sleep time, rebalancing your energy and eliminating any health problems. And who knows—if you use these psychic sleep techniques, you may be more intuitive during the day as well!

You already know that when it comes to your psychic ability, you should always do what feels right to you, and this is especially true when it comes to your sleep. The best way to use your sleep in a psychic way to rebalance and restore your health is actually to experiment with several different exercises in this book, and to integrate your own affirmations and visualizations and figure out what works best for you. If your mind is actively trying to follow certain steps to the letter, or you are doing an exercise that I recommend but finding it ineffective, you'll probably find yourself more awake than when you got into bed.

If you have insomnia or any other sleeping problem, I have provided a helpful exercise to discover the source of the problem and get rid of it. Also remember that if you have insomnia or you find yourself sleeping a lot, it doesn't necessarily mean something is wrong with you. When you start developing your connection to psychic energy, all sorts of extraordinary things happen. Sometimes I go through periods where I sleep a lot; sometimes I have so much energy that I wake up for a few hours in the middle of the night with an extremely strong desire to write, meditate, or talk to my angels—then I go back to sleep. I've learned to listen to my body and not to force things. If your patterns start becoming unpredictable, that very well could be your psychic side asserting itself.

When I am overexcited and can't get to sleep, I like to surround myself with a shield of protection, and call in the angels in charge of sleeping (yes, there are angels that help us to fall asleep!). I concentrate on sleeping, and that somehow works like a charm. Try this; you may find that a moment with your angels is a very effective sleep aid!

Psychic Workout
Getting a Good Psychic Sleep

There are several exercises in this book that you can do lying down in bed to balance your energy as you sleep. Try each of these for a few days, and you'll begin to see what works best for you:

- *Relaxing (chapter 1)*
- *In and Up (chapter 2)*
- *Grounding (chapter 2)*
- *Rebalance Your Energy, Restore Your Health (this chapter)*

Using these workouts to fall asleep is similar to the way you use them during your psychic session. If you are not that familiar with these exercises, you may have to read the instructions several times before you go to sleep, so your mind will not draw a blank while you are drifting off to sleep.

Adding some affirmations and visualizations to these exercises will also help you to fall asleep. Try sending the affirmation "Sleep" to each part of your body. Slowly repeat the word "sleep" in your head, as the universal energy flows through your body. You might find a word that works better for you, such as "release" or "calm."

Visualizations will also ease you into a deep sleep. If you like the water, visualize yourself floating on calm, deep, blue water as you do one of these exercises. If you enjoy nature, visualize yourself lying on a mattress in a meadow or forest. Remember our brief discussion of color in chapter 1 when choosing candles? The colors that will be most helpful for you to use when you are trying to sleep are: deep blue for calming, green for healing, and deep purple for intuition. I suggest you stay away from visualizing yellow, orange, and red. They are stimulating, active colors that might serve to wake you up rather than put you to sleep. You can use these colors however you like, visualizing them in calming pictures or imagining just one as you breathe deeply in and out in a deep meditative state.

When you've had a particularly stressful day, you may find these exercises aren't strong enough to relax you into a calm sleep. In that case, grab the notebook you keep in bed and write down everything that your mind is focused on. Write and write—get the stuff out of your head. Promise yourself you're not going to think about it again until the morning, and then try one of the exercises I just mentioned. You should be so exhausted by this time that you pass out at some point before you finish the workout.

If you're having a problem falling asleep and don't find any of these exercises effective, it could be that your insomnia is a sign that something is off balance in your body or your belief system. That is where a little investigation comes in handy. If your insomnia keeps happening, pick an exercise from chapter 4 and ask yourself some questions:

Why am I not sleeping?
What is the issue behind this insomnia?

What do I need to know about this insomnia?
What can I do to sleep better?

You may find that you are not getting enough exercise or exercising too late in the evening. You may find that avoiding certain foods or not speaking on the phone right before you go to sleep will enable you to sleep more soundly. Once you pinpoint exactly why you are not sleeping and what you can be doing to alleviate the problem, take the appropriate steps, and the problem should go away after a few days. If you find your sleeping problem is a symptom of a larger issue, then use the exercise most appropriate to examine the issue further.

Eating for Your Psychic Well-being

Maintaining optimal health also means creating and eating the perfect foods for you. With all the studies out there about what to eat and what not to eat, eating for your health isn't that easy. You are not going to find your best eating habits in a book or a medical study. The only way you are going to find an eating plan that is perfect for you is to listen to your body and your guides and develop a healthy eating plan from the inside out: a plan that will keep your energy high, your resilience up, and your body functioning up to par.

Everyone has within them a perfect eating plan. Using your connection to psychic energy to discover what you should eat will enable you to find peace with what you put in your mouth, and will help you achieve your health and weight goals. You may discover that you should be eating fruit salad for lunch; or that you shouldn't eat potatoes and bread after 7 P.M. If you listen to your body, you will never be hungry, and your body will never feel deprived.

Here is my own inner food plan, which has helped me balance my weight and energy over the past seven years. First, I became a vegetar-

Psychic Vitamin Pill

You don't have to wait until you're sick to use the universal energy to improve your health. No matter how good you feel, you can strengthen your good health by doing some psychic visualizations along with your other exercises. It's like your own personal psychic vitamin pill.

The best exercise to anchor perfect health is Becoming Comfortable with Your Destiny (chapter 3). Let's go over the details as they pertain to perfect health. Begin by creating your sacred space and getting into a deep meditative state. If you want to do a mini session, skip the sacred space and take a deep breath instead. Create a pod and size it to fit snugly around you. Create an optimally healthy, energized, and vital You inside the pod. Infuse it with all the feelings and thoughts that you have at your physical peak. Verbally describe what you see and feel. When you are ready, pull the pod around you, becoming the Perfect You.

You can also add power to the pod exercise by using Affirmations and Visualizations daily (chapter 3). Create a list of affirmative phrases and visual images that will anchor good health into your reality. Affirm: *I am strong* or *I live with great health and vitality.* And visualize images of yourself with powerful universal energy flowing through you. Add the Put an Angel on Your Shoulder exercise from chapter 8. Having an angel watch over you with a little added protection will enable you to feel safe and secure while living in perfect health.

ian. I never felt like my body metabolized meat very well, so I just gave it up altogether. Then, with the universe's assistance, I established some parameters for eating. I got into a meditative state and asked my guides to help me create good eating habits. What I received from them was a plan I could follow that would keep me healthy and trim without constantly wanting more food.

Each day, I basically eat one meal of fruit (breakfast), one meal of vegetables or salad, and two or three meals of whatever I want except foods on my "no-no" list. The no-no list includes fattening and unhealthy stuff like fried foods, pizza, or big desserts. I eat a total of four or five small meals each day, never eating so much that I feel bloated and slowed down. The best part of the plan: As long as I follow it four out of five days each week, I can guiltlessly go off it once or twice a week and not think twice! I can eat pizza or a big ice cream sundae every now and then without any guilt.

My guides knew the exact right plan that would satisfy me emotionally and physically. By asking them to work with me and set up the best plan for me, I have found a lifetime's worth of good health and weight fulfillment. I know you will find the plan that is perfect for you!

Psychic Workout
Discovering a Healthy Eating and Exercise Plan

Discovering your perfect eating and exercise plan is a matter of some easy inner research. Take out your notebook and write down a few appropriate questions. Here are some good ones:

What do I need to know about my eating habits?
What is the best food plan for my optimal health?
What foods should I avoid eating?
How can I best put this plan into action every day?
What type of exercise would comfortably fit into my schedule?
What is the best exercise schedule for me?

Choose one of the information-gathering exercises from chapter 4 and receive the answers to your questions. As you put the plan into action, you may find that you need to make adjustments to your daily eating habits until you figure out exactly what works. If this is the case, check in with the universe every couple of days or weeks and ask how you are doing. You also may find that your eating and exercise habits change as your psychic ability develops. Whenever you feel unsatisfied with the foods you are eating or the exercise you are doing, do this workout again and develop a new food and exercise plan.

Healthy Beliefs Create Healthy Lives

Whether you're always healthy, you get occasional colds or aches, or you suffer from a chronic illness, having an empowering belief system is the foundation of good health.

We originally discussed belief systems back in chapter 3. A belief system is a group of thoughts we hold about reality that dictates the way we operate in the world. Some of these beliefs can be negative and therefore limit the success we can have in all areas of our lives. When we examine these core beliefs, we see what we are operating with. Once they are out in the open, we are able to mold and change them to create a better foundation for our future.

Does your belief system allow you to operate fully with optimum health? A fully empowered healthy belief system has two core values:

1. A belief that health is our natural state of being.
2. A belief that we have within us the power to fix any health problem and restore ourselves to a naturally healthy state.

If you have these two beliefs in your system, you will not only perpetuate your good health, you will be able to heal quickly and easily when you do have a problem. Before you can access your body's natural healing powers, you first have to examine your belief system by doing the following workout. If you find that you have any problems believing and completely trusting these two core belief statements, do the suggested psychic homework to give these beliefs power and strength in your life. Once these powerful thoughts are operating in your life, you will feel more energetic, suffer fewer colds and other minor ailments, and be able to access your natural healing abilities to heal from illnesses quickly.

Psychic Workout
Examining Your Health Beliefs

To find out if you have a positive health belief system, take stock of your beliefs about your health. Begin by taking out your notebook and writing a few questions, leaving space for the answers. A few good questions are:

What are my beliefs about my health?
What are my fears about my health?
How much do I believe in my powers of self-healing?
How much do I believe in my perfect health as a natural state?

Do the Fears and Beliefs workout in chapter 3 and receive the answers to your questions. Beliefs aren't black or white. You may find that you believe in both core beliefs to a certain degree or believe in one more strongly than the other. If this is the case, work with the universal energy and the power of your mind to strengthen those two beliefs within yourself.

Do the Becoming Comfortable with Your Destiny workout (chapter 3) and visualize yourself free from illness. See your body's natural systems working to balance your health. Know that your optimal health is within your power. Do affirmations as well; create powerful positive statements that will help you release your negative health beliefs and fully empower your beliefs about your health. Try statements such as: I believe in my own power to heal; I believe in my good health. *After a few weeks of doing this inner homework, you'll find you have stronger health and vitality. You will also find that you heal more quickly and easily.*

Understanding Your Health from the Inside Out

Now that you've worked on correcting your belief system, you can move on to better understanding the psychic side of your health. After doing the previous workout, you may have discovered that you basically believe the two core beliefs for good health, yet you're wondering why you still get the occasional cold. You might have discovered that your beliefs in the areas of your health needed some work, but you still have to get rid of that backache or stomach problem.

Chances are that no matter how strong your health beliefs are, you still may get sick on occasion. Health problems are the result of an imbalance in the connection of body, mind, and, soul. You may have worked on balancing your energy today, but as you live your life, you may find that a certain situation can cause you to learn new things about yourself and throw off your belief system. That is when you may develop a health problem.

It's like a car. Even a car that runs well may get out of whack and need a tuneup or realignment every so often. By better understanding all the possible reasons for a health condition and knowing how to get right to the root of the problem, you can psychically work on eliminating it and bring your health beliefs back into alignment again.

I believe there are four underlying reasons for health problems.

1. You may develop an illness if you are meant to learn something from it on a soul level. *In other words, an illness may be helping you learn a lesson or how to overcome adversity.*

2. Your illness may be directly related to your karma. *If your marriage in your last life revolved around you taking care of your sick mate, you may end up experiencing the exact same illness in your present life in order to understand both perspectives.*

3. Your illness may have come about due to an imbalance of energy in your life. *If you are unhappy with some aspects of your life and are not addressing the negativity, it can be released in your body as a way of finding balance.*

4. You may have too many negative thoughts in your belief system. *Strong negative thoughts about your health or a deep-seated belief that you will never feel well will create poor health.*

No matter what the cause of your illness, there is a way to use your psychic powers to overcome it. By going within and using psychic energy to identify what you are learning from an illness, what belief is causing it, or what karma is being balanced, you can address and heal the problem.

Let's look more deeply into each of these possible reasons for ill health:

1. Learning Lessons. *Your health problem is helping teach you a lesson. For example, you may need to learn a lesson about unconditional love. If you are ill and have to be taken care of by another person for a while, chances are, you will experience unconditional love. The severity of the health problem relates to the difficulty of the lesson.*

2. Karma. *Remember karma, from chapter 5? Karma is the force behind the actions and reactions we experience that teach us right from wrong. Maybe you were a teacher in another life and you disciplined your students by smacking a ruler across their hands. You may find that the arthritis you have in your fingers in this life is directly related to that action. Karma isn't always past-life oriented. Any powerful lesson you choose to overcome in this lifetime is made up of a series of actions and reactions. Maybe you have a hard time dealing with your anger, and every time you get very angry and yell at someone, you get a sore throat.*

3. An imbalance of energy in your life. *If you don't let go of negative feelings and emotions, they will end up being released through your body, causing pain or illness. Say, for example, you dislike your boss and you get anxiety-ridden every time you have meetings with him. If you don't release*

that anxiety, one day it will take its toll on your body, causing anything from a simple cold to an accident in which you get a broken arm.

4. Negative beliefs regarding your health. *I have one client who is in perfect health but is sure that one day she is going to get a disease. Every time I see her, she asks me the same questions about her health. This constant bombardment of negative thoughts leaves her susceptible to the very problem she is afraid of.*

This last reason looks like it conflicts with the positive beliefs you laid down as your foundation in the previous section. This is not the case. Our belief systems are incredibly intricate, made up of many, many beliefs, some of them conflicting. You can easily believe in your natural state of good health and still have some negative belief residue about certain areas of your body or develop a problem as you learn certain lessons, as I mentioned earlier.

Once you understand the different reasons for health problems that may arise in your life, you are equipped with the knowledge you need to get right to the root of the issue. Understanding the different causes of ill health will help you map out the steps you need to take to get back to good health. The following psychic exercise is designed to pinpoint underlying problems and discover appropriate actions to take toward good health.

I use the healing process in the next exercise all the time. One day I woke up feeling lousy, and I sat down with my notebook and used the Communicating with the Universe workout (chapter 4) to get to the bottom of what was wrong with me. First I wrote a short description of the problem: *My stomach aches and my left knee hurts.* I got into a meditative state and asked my body what the underlying issues were. Here is the answer I received:

My stomach aches from the energy being drained by a misunderstanding with my parents.
My left knee hurts—it's a sympathy pain for my friend who recently underwent a painful knee operation.

When I asked what I could do to fix the problems, I got this response:

Release the emotional trauma of the misunderstanding. Fill and restore energy to your solar plexus.

Surround yourself with a protective bubble of universal energy to protect yourself from others' pain.

During my weekly psychic sessions, I use the Rebalance Your Energy, Restore Your Health exercise to restore my energy, as well as the Put an Angel on Your Shoulder mini workout (chapter 8). These techniques have worked very well, and I have been having fewer stomachaches since I received this information.

Psychic Workout
Understanding Your Health and Releasing the Problem

Take out your notebook and write a short description of the health issue you wish to look into. Then write a few appropriate questions. Here are some good questions to ask:

What is the reason for this health problem?
How can I better understand this health issue?
What beliefs do I have regarding this health issue?
Is this health problem the result of some karmic action?

Pick one of the information-gathering exercises from chapter 4, create your sacred space, and get the answers to your questions. Once you understand the origins of your health issue, again get into a meditative state. This time ask the universe for the actions you can take to help yourself. Here are some good questions to ask:

What steps can I take back to health?
What can I do to release this illness and heal myself?

End your session as instructed in the specific exercise you chose. Then follow the actions you discovered during the exercise.

In addition to taking the appropriate actions, use your psychic sessions to work with the universal energy and release the problem. The Rebalance Your Energy, Restore Your Health workout (this chapter) is a great exercise for doing this type of healing work. Use the Becoming Comfortable with Your Destiny exercise (chapter 3) to focus on good health, and try Magnetizing Your Goals (chapter 4) to magnetize good health.

Depending on what category you find your health problem falling into, do these additional exercises:

- *If your health problem relates to a lesson you are learning: Do any of the information-gathering exercises from chapter 4 and ask yourself what this problem is teaching you.*
- *If your health problem relates to karma: Do the exercises in understanding and transcending karma (chapter 5) to release the issue from your life.*
- *If your problem stems from an imbalance in your energy or you have negative thoughts about your health: Do the Fears and Beliefs exercise (chapter 3) to discover exactly what fears and negative beliefs you are holding about your health. As the exercise instructs, create a list of positive beliefs to study.*

AT A GLANCE
Understanding Your Health and Releasing the Problem

Step One Take out your notebook and write appropriate questions designed to get to the reasons behind your health problem.

Step Two Using one of the information-gathering exercises from chapter 4, receive the answers to your questions.

Step Three Again get into a meditative state, this time asking for concrete actions you can take to alleviate the problem.

Step Four Close your sacred space. Then follow the action you were given, and incorporate relevant exercises listed earlier.

Getting Rid of Aches and Pains

You're at the office, with a screaming headache. You woke up with a stiff neck. You've had a gnawing stomachache all day and can't figure out why. Many of us have minor aches and pains that pop up as we go about our day. But even though these aches and pains may be symptoms of a deeper health issue—as I just discussed—there is no reason to let pain get in the way of your daily activities. You can release symptoms of discomfort without having to get to the root of the underlying problem at that very moment. When you're busy, your psychic ability will fit into your schedule, and not the other way around! When you

Want to Use Your Sleep Constructively? Program Your Dreams!

Do you want to know what the outcome of a tricky situation will be or how you can best resolve a problem? Use your sleep time as receiving time. Right before you go to bed at night or take a nap, write in your notebook a short description of the problem you are experiencing and ask what the outcome will be or how to best handle the situation. Take a moment to ask your spirit guides and angels to help you get the answers you are looking for. Put your notebook near where you sleep (don't forget a pen!). The answer will probably just pop into your head before you fall asleep, during a dream, or as you wake up. Capture the solution you need by writing it down quickly before you get out of bed.

have a headache in the middle of the day, you might not have time to get into a deep meditative state and ask for the reason behind it as you did in the earlier workout. Most important, you want to get rid of the headache so you can get back to work.

There is a special thirty-second mini session you can do to release pain so you can go on with the rest of your day. But because you are releasing symptoms and not the cause, you may find that later in the day you get another ache or pain. In that case, repeat the exercise steps again. Later, when it's more convenient, get into a deep state and ask yourself some questions to get to the root of the problem and what you can do to heal it. Once you get to the bottom of the imbalance and take steps to alleviate the problem, your ache will have gotten its point across, and you will still have had a fulfilling day.

When I get a minor ache or pain, I like to surround myself with a protective shield, call in all the angels in charge of healing, and ask them to work on the area that hurts—like a celestial massage. Try it!

Psychic Workout
Getting Rid of Unexpected Pain

If you have some minor ache or pain, give yourself a few minutes; then find a quiet place—in your work cubicle, the bathroom, a hallway. Close your eyes, and get into a deep state by breathing a few times. Repeat this phrase several times:

Ache, I release you. I release you.

Then visualize the universal energy washing over your body like a shower, washing away blocked or negative energy and cleansing the area that hurts. Then picture pure white universal energy filling the space with its healing qualities. This should take about thirty seconds. Thank the universe for taking the pain away, and go on with the rest of your day.

Whenever it's more convenient—on a lunch break, on the train, or when you get home—go back to Understanding Your Health and Releasing the Problem and ask yourself the reasons for your pain and what you can do to get rid of it. Once you get to the bottom of the imbalance, take the appropriate actions to resolve it. You can also do these other thirty-second to one-minute workouts to heal your aches and pains:

Grounding (chapter 2)
Relaxing (chapter 2)
Put an Angel on Your Shoulder (chapter 8)

AT A GLANCE
Getting Rid of Unexpected Pain

Step One Find a quiet place, close your eyes, and get into a deep state.

Step Two Repeat the releasing phrase several times: "Ache, I release you. I release you."

Step Three Visualize universal energy washing over your body, washing away blocked or negative energy and cleansing the area that hurts.

Step Four Picture pure white universal energy filling the space where your pain once was. Thank the universe for taking the pain away.

Step Five Whenever it's convenient, use one of the information-gathering exercises from chapter 4 to ask the universe why the pain occurred and what you can do to rid yourself of it. Take the appropriate actions.

Let Dr. Universe Treat Your Health Problem

When you have a health concern, whether it is a cold, a lack of energy, a broken bone, or an ongoing illness, you can work on releasing it yourself as you did with the previous exercise. You can also use your connection to your spirit guides and angels to fix the problem. Angels and guides are great for creating miracles in your life. By working with them to rid yourself of a problem, you separate yourself from the problem and enable the universe to heal it for you.

The following exercise is designed to be an intimate exchange between you and the universe: your guides, angels, and Higher Self. By talking directly with the universe and giving it your illness, you allow it to give you back your health. It is a simple energy exchange.

If you have a health problem, you can do this exercise along with all the other things you are doing to rid yourself of the problem: workouts like Rebalance Your Energy, Restore Your Health or Becoming Comfortable with Your Destiny.

Psychic Workout
Transcending Health Problems

Begin by getting into a deep meditative state. Create a ball of light about four feet above you and a few feet in front of you, so that you can see it with your inner vision without any discomfort to your neck. This ball of light is the purest source of universal energy—your angels, spirit guides, Higher Self, or God. This should take no more than fifteen seconds.

When you are ready, repeat this short statement several times with all of the intention in your soul:

Dear Spirit, I release this illness to you. I release this illness to you. Give me back my health. Heal my body, mind, and soul. I am in perfect health.

As you repeat this phrase, visually hand your illness or pain to the ball of light. Give the problem to the universe and let it fix the problem for you; visualize the universe handing back to you perfect health. Remind yourself that you no longer have this illness. Do this several times a day until you feel relief. After each time you do this, know *that the illness is gone.*

AT A GLANCE
Transcending Health Problems

Step One Get into a deep meditative state.

Step Two Create a ball of light about four feet above you and a few feet in front of you, so that you can see it with your inner vision without any discomfort to your neck.

Step Three Repeat the following statement several times with all of the intention in your soul: "Dear Spirit, I release this illness to you. I release this illness to you. Give me back my health. Heal my body, mind, and soul. I am in perfect health." As you do this, visually hand your illness to the ball of light. Visualize the universe handing back to you perfect health.

Have a Sick Friend, Family Member, or Pet?
Send 'Em Some Healing!

You don't have to be near the ones you love in order to help them heal; you can do so anytime, anyplace, anywhere! Take a moment, close your eyes, and create an open channel between you and your sick loved one—from your heart to his or her heart. Then open a channel from the top of your head into the universe. Using your body as a conduit, pull down the energy from the universe and send it through your heart to your friend. Send pure loving thoughts along with the energy.

Physical Appearance

Appearances are ultra-important in the world we live in. Good or bad, that's the way it is. And because of that, many of us dislike parts of our appearance: our weight, our height, our body shape. While we may be genetically predisposed to certain physical characteristics, there is no reason we can't work with them to become happier with who we are. When you and everyone in your family are five-five, I'm not saying you can become six-one, but certain aspects of your appearance you definitely can control. And when I say control, I don't mean diet like crazy and make yourself sick; I mean you can use the power of your mind to create wonderful changes. You can lose inches around your waist, make yourself appear taller, balance your skin tone, fill out your butt—whatever.

This section is devoted to exercises and techniques that can help you change anything and everything about your appearance that you wish to. Lose a few pounds, take a few inches off your thighs, add an inch to your height—if you can think of it, you can make it happen. You may think it is impossible to use some intangible energy to effectively change your concrete physical characteristics, but I assure you, nothing is impossible when it comes to the power of psychic energy.

It's important to remember that sometimes what we see with our eyes is an illusion. By working on changing your appearance from the inside out, you shift the work to a deeper, more powerful place: a place that knows only the limitations that you put on yourself. As your inner reality shifts, your outer reality shifts. That is the philosophy behind this section. By using the power of your mind, you mold your reality to fit your desires. It all starts in your head.

There are two exercises to change your physical appearance in this section. One is geared toward changing any characteristics of your body that you wish to—chest, hands, waist, hips; the other is geared specifically toward losing and gaining weight. Although weight is just another of our physical characteristics, I wanted to give it special attention, since for many of us weight affects our moods and our very outlook on life, not to mention our health. And psychically, there are different ways of handling it.

Changing Specific Parts of Your Body

Do you wish your thighs were thinner or your skin tone more balanced? Do you want to be taller or have thicker hair? There's no reason you have to accept anything about your body that you don't like. When you use your powerful connection to the universe to change specific parts of your body, you use the power of your mind to become what you want to be. By using your inner senses to focus on visual images, you enable your physical characteristics to change to match the picture.

No matter how much brain power you use, the universe is the ultimate source. By using the universe as your tool, you change for the better, but you may not exactly know what that will be. If you have deep red hair, you may not be able to change your hair color to light blond, but you will be able to get a more golden color—a color that is perfectly beautiful on you.

As the universe helps you alter your appearance, you may be surprised at what you see. It is very simple to use psychic energy to change your appearance, but it is just as easy to become more comfortable with your current appearance using psychic energy. I'm not saying you should compromise what you want and learn to be happy with it. I am saying that once you work with the universe to change your physical body, you change something even deeper than that. You may see some physical characteristics change right before your eyes. You may see some discomfort with your appearance wash away. Or you may find that your energy changes so that people perceive you differently.

There are three parts to the following exercise:

1. *Examining your beliefs about different body parts*
2. *Getting rid of any negativity you may be holding onto*
3. *Using the universe to change those parts*

Because this exercise works by creating inner pictures of what the outer you will look like, you must first reexamine your inner tools—your thoughts and beliefs about the areas of your body you wish to change. If your tools are broken, you must fix them before you will see any physical changes in your body. Then you are ready to create the changes you wish to see, using the universal energy to create and affirm the inner visual images that will soon become your outer physical image.

Psychic Workout
Changing Physical Characteristics

Begin by taking out your notebook and writing a short list of the parts of your body you wish to change. You may wish you had a smaller nose, fewer wrinkles around your eyes, or thicker hair. Once your list is complete, do the What's Not Working in Your Life exercise (chapter 3) and discover what your limiting thoughts and beliefs are about each of the things on your list.

After you have assessed your beliefs and fears regarding specific parts of your body, clear away any negativity you may have by creating a list of Affirmations and Visualizations (chapter 3) that will help you eliminate this negativity from your belief system. Stop here. Do these affirmations and visualizations for a week or two before going on to the rest of the exercise.

At this point you should have cleared away any debris that may be getting in the way of changing the specific areas of your body. Now you are ready to create the changes you wish to see. The best exercise to use is Becoming Comfortable with Your Destiny (chapter 3). During that exercise, you create a pod with a perfect You in it, and you pull the pod around you, becoming the perfect You. As you create the perfect You in the pod, see yourself physically as you wish to be, with your ideal height, hair, skin, fingernails, and so on. Now visualize whatever changes you wish to make. If you are changing more than one area of your body, make sure you fully visualize the first change before going on to the next. Infuse the You in the pod with all the inspired feelings of love and happiness that you experience as you feel these changes occurring in your body.

You can also do the Magnetizing Your Goals workout (chapter 4). Visually attract to yourself all the physical characteristics you wish to have. Visually imagine yourself living with these characteristics. Do either or both of these workouts three times a day for about three minutes each session; soon you'll begin to live the perfect You. You should see changes within a day or a week—unless other people notice them first!

AT A GLANCE
Changing Physical Characteristics

Step One Take out your notebook and write a short list of the parts of your body that you wish to change.

Step Two Discover what your limiting thoughts and beliefs are about each item on the list by using the What's Not Working in Your Life exercise.

Step Three Clear away any negativity you find by creating and repeating a list of affirmations and visualizations.

Step Four Create change in your specific body parts by working through the Becoming Comfortable with Your Destiny workout and the Magnetizing Your Goals workout.

Losing or Gaining Weight in a Psychic State

For most of us, weight is the physical characteristic that preoccupies us the most. We want to lose it, we want to gain it, we want to round out our curves, we want to define our muscles. We want to look and feel better in and out of our clothes. With the help of the universe, you will no longer have to struggle with your weight. You can actually use psychic energy to think yourself to weight perfection.

I think that the issue of weight is completely misunderstood and misrepresented in our society. We're taught that to get control over our weight we have to diet like crazy, exercise our tails off, take pills, drink shakes, down tons of vitamins, pump iron, drink herbal teas, and do a host of other things short of standing on our heads while singing "The Star-Spangled Banner." All this stuff bombarding us can make the most normal human very neurotic about his or her weight!

Basically what that stuff is telling us is that we cannot control our weight and body image without the help of something outside of us. But from a psychic perspective, there is nothing in life that you don't have, and can't get, control over. You may not have consciously decided to be too heavy or too thin, but somewhere along the line, you unconsciously let go of your control over the issue. Maybe you have negative thoughts about your weight in your belief system, or maybe you are karmically dealing with weight issues as life lessons. Whatever the reasons, you can use psychic energy to get to the bottom of your weight issues, take appropriate actions, regain control, and eliminate a weight problem from your life.

In a nutshell, working with the universe to change your weight goes like this: You assess your thoughts about your weight and your control over how you look. Then you use the power of the universe to restructure those thoughts, reconstructing You physically. That enables you to fundamentally let go of your body image as you know it and create a whole new way of looking at yourself.

When you use your psychic ability to lose or gain weight, you first must address the root causes of the problem. Whether it is a lesson you are learning or an issue you are overcoming, getting to the root of the issue will enable you to eliminate it from your life. This involves taking stock of what's in your head by examining the issues, lessons, fears, and beliefs that make up your belief system about your weight. It might not be easy to examine the issues and beliefs that are causing your discomfort, but it must be done in order to see what may be stopping you from being content with your weight. When you discover the deep-seated issues, fears, and beliefs you may be holding about your body, your weight, and your relationship with food, you will see what's in the way of getting where you want to be.

When you look into your limiting beliefs, fears, and unresolved issues about weight, you may find that you may think you want to lose ten pounds, but underneath it all you feel that you cannot deal with the world without a buffer of flesh. You may feel that even if you did lose ten pounds, there is no way you'll ever keep off the extra weight—it will come back in a matter of time. You may believe what I believed ten years ago, that you are just one of those unlucky people who have to starve in order to be thin. Maybe you'll discover that you have an underlying issue that is not about food and you must free yourself of an even *more* deep-seated problem. In that case, by exploring it you may find peace without needing to get rid of an extra ten pounds. When you clear yourself of your inner baggage, you will naturally look and feel your perfect weight.

After you've gotten to your core issues and negative beliefs, the next step is to work on shedding any negativity you may have found. Ten years ago, when I was heavier and miserable with my body, I had a very different set of beliefs about my weight than I do today. Let's analyze what changes occurred between my being the unhappy overweight person I was, on and off after my freshman year in college, and being the empowered psychic that I am today.

First, my beliefs. When I was twenty pounds heavier, the beliefs that permeated my belief system were: *I am one of those people with a slow metabolism. If I want to lose weight and keep it off, I have to eat very little. I will never be able to eat what I want and be happy.* Quite negative and limiting, wouldn't you say? Now my beliefs about my weight are much different. I believe that I can basically eat what I want and not gain weight. I also feel that my metabolism is strong as long as I work out regularly.

These beliefs changed as I changed inside my head. As I began fulfilling my destiny as a psychic, I gradually forgot about my body issues. The miserable neurotic dieter was replaced with a balanced and fulfilled Me who was free from any constraints. The new thoughts made a new reality.

After you have shed negativity, you are free to use the universal energy to create the You you want to be. This does not mean you have to accept the weight you are now; it means using your mind to become thin or curvy or free of the issue altogether. I *know* this works; my first manager and friend, Theresa, psychically thought off six pounds doing the following exercises without making any changes in her eating habits whatsoever. She didn't feel deprived or hungry. She didn't even notice she had lost weight until people around her started to comment that she looked thin.

The key to enlisting the help of the universe to resolve your weight issues *permanently* is to set up a comfortable eating plan and to commit to following that plan. Review the Eating for Your Psychic Wellbeing section and set up a perfect eating plan for You. Although setting up a healthy eating plan is one thing and following it is another, you can help yourself by doing frequent psychic sessions to connect with the universe and by asking your guides and angels to help you tweak your food plan until it is comfortable and satisfying.

This is not a quick fix like a shake or a pill; this is your eating plan for a healthy life. So even though you will feel and see improvements immediately, it may take a few weeks to months for the tweaking process to remove any discomfort, dissatisfaction, or deprivation you may experience. Since you are in this thing for the long haul, think of it as time well spent!

This exercise is not about setting up a diet but rather about using universal energy to change your body image and weight. Establishing a healthy eating plan is the appropriate action that will assist your mind in creating these changes. The process works from the inside out; your mind creates the changes, not your mouth.

A helpful tip for those of you who wish to gain or lose more than ten pounds or more than one or two sizes: It may not be within your reality zone to drop forty pounds and three clothes sizes or gain four inches and plenty of muscle all at once. Think about working in increments. A goal has to be reachable in order for the work in this book to succeed, so do these exercises ten pounds or one clothing size at a time. You may not be able to visualize yourself losing forty pounds, but you can see yourself losing ten. You may not see how your bony chest can be swelling with muscle, but you can imagine your shoulders with a bit more brawn. This way, you'll always be working within your reality zone and always working toward your goal!

Psychic Workout
Losing or Gaining Weight

Before you can get where you want to be, you must first take stock of what got you to this point. Do so by taking out your notebook and writing some questions. Here are some good ones:

What are my fears about my weight?
What are my beliefs about my weight?
What is stopping me from being happy with my weight?
What is stopping me from being the weight I wish to be?
Why am I so unhappy with my weight?
What do I need to learn by being at this weight?

To get the answers to these questions, choose one of the information-gathering exercises from chapter 4:

- Communicating with the Universe
- Finding Your Psychic Solution
- Magnetizing Information

Since there are two questions on the list that are directly related to fears and beliefs, you can also do the Fears and Beliefs workout (chapter 3) to get answers.

Using the exercise you chose, get into a meditative state and receive the answers to your questions. After you've gotten to the core issues, the next step is to work on shedding any negativity that you may have discovered: unresolved weight issues, lessons you are learning, fears, and beliefs. Start with Affirmations and Visualizations (chapter 3). Write a list of affirmations that counterbalance the negative beliefs in your belief system. Create visualizations that free you from your weight limitations. Write a new set of beliefs to replace the old ones (using Fears and Beliefs). These words and inner visions will fuel your new belief system, which will in turn become a solid foundation for a thin and carefree You.

After you have shed negativity, you are free to use the universal energy to create the You you want to be. The best exercise for losing and gaining weight is the Becoming Comfortable with Your Destiny workout (chapter 3). During that exercise you create a pod with a perfect You in it, and pull the pod around you, becoming the perfect You. As you create the perfect You in the pod, see yourself physically as you wish to be, with your ideal weight and measurements. Now visualize whatever changes you wish to make. If you are changing more than one area of your body, make sure you fully visualize the first change before going on to the next. Infuse the You in the pod with all the inspired feelings of love and happiness that you experience as you feel these changes occurring in your body. Do this at least twice a day for three or four minutes, and you will begin to see changes within a few days.

Finally, set up a comfortable eating plan by using the Discover a Healthy Eating and Exercise Plan exercise. It may take several psychic sessions and a few weeks of trial and error to bang out a plan that you are comfortable with and can stick to. When you first complete the Discover a Healthy Eating and Exercise Plan exercise you'll find yourself asking questions like: "What foods should I be eating to maximize my energy and achieve my goals?" As the weeks go by, you may find yourself asking different questions, such as: "When is the best time for me to snack?" "How come I want to eat more of this particular food?" or: "What is the perfect amount of this food for me?"

As you take these last action-oriented steps, concentrate on visual images of the perfect You in the Becoming Comfortable with Your Destiny exercise until the new food plan is anchored in your everyday life and you have completely changed your mental body image. This change may take three daily sessions of three to four minutes each for a number of months, but once it occurs, your new weight will feel comfortable and sustainable.

AT A GLANCE
Losing or Gaining Weight

Step One Look into your fears and beliefs about food and weight. Write appropriate questions in your notebook.

Step Two Using one of the information-gathering exercises from chapter 4, get into a meditative state and receive the answers to your questions.

Step Three Create affirmations and visualizations to help yourself shed the negative beliefs you just discovered.

Step Four Begin to use the universal energy to change your body. Do the Becoming Comfortable with Your Destiny workout, focusing on your body and weight.

Step Five Set up a comfortable eating plan by following the Discover a Healthy Eating and Exercise Plan workout.

Step Six Follow that plan, taking the next action to bring you closer to your goals.

You can absolutely look and feel as good as you want, and the universe is here to help. Remember, the most important part of this work is making yourself feel better, whether it's getting rid of chronic pain, losing weight, or becoming comfortable with your body exactly the way it is. The more you use your body as a channel for psychic energy, the more your natural health and beauty resonate from within you. Then you, as well as others, will find you irresistible—both inside and out.

chapter eight

happiness

———

After I graduated from college, I went straight to work at MTV. I had a great job, the envy of all the people I'd gone to college with who were now suffering through entry-level jobs as management trainees and paralegals. For nearly four years, I worked my way up from production assistant to writer and associate producer.

I was always in the middle of the excitement, and I was *very* stressed out. I found all the distraction oddly pacifying. In the beginning it had been thrilling, but after a year or two I was working because I didn't know any better. I was always on automatic pilot; I didn't have time to stop and think about the direction my life was going. I was pretty much nonexistent in my own mind. The questions I asked myself back then were more about fulfilling others' expectations of me than what I wanted for myself. "How *should* I feel about this? What *should* I do? Where *should* I be?"

Then MTV canceled the show I was working on, and I joined the ranks of the unemployed. For the first time in my life I had nothing to do but sit and think. I thought a lot about what I perceived as my failure in my career and my unhappiness until it dawned on me that I was only a failure in my own mind. I had been competing against myself.

I decided to take the next year and devote it to doing whatever *I* wanted to do. I took some acting classes, studied the tarot, began doing standup comedy, and took plenty of odd jobs in order to make ends meet. At the end of that year I still didn't go out and find a *real* job—I got work as an extra in movies; I performed at fledgling comedy shows; and I gave tarot card readings at parties. I found freedom, and I haven't looked back since.

That experience taught me many lessons. The first thing I learned is that you can be young for a lot longer than you think you can. When

The Ten Best Paranormal Newspaper Headlines

One "Chatty Spirit Guide Accidentally Reveals Colonel Sanders's Secret Recipe"

Two "Pathfinder Probe Finds Elvis Living on Mars"

Three "Washing Machine's Spin Cycle Found Responsible for Sending Socks into Fourth Dimension"

Four "Psychic Sues Boss for Sexual Harassment. Files Suit in Advance, Citing Long Delays in Court Process"

Five "Ghost of Christmas Past Discusses Time Travel"

Six "Top Pool Player Disqualified for Mistakenly Shooting Magic 8-Ball into Corner Pocket"

Seven "Psychic Arrested for Shoplifting; Says Sale Items Followed Her out of Store"

Eight "Aliens Found in 7-Eleven, Exploring Phenomenon We Call 'Slurpee'"

Nine "Levitating Psychic Has Near-death Experience Hitting Traffic Light during Morning Commute"

Ten "Famous Psychic Predicted This Headline Would Run Last Week"

I left MTV, my initial reaction was that I was washed up at age twenty-five. Now I joke about how I've matured into my youth—and I'm really enjoying it! I also learned that you can do anything you want to do; as long as you do it with all your heart and soul, you'll find success within yourself and in the world. Once I began shedding my view of myself as an unemployed television producer and began thinking of myself as a psychic-actress-comedian, a whole new world opened up in front of my eyes.

This change didn't happen overnight; it took two or three years until I finally focused on my destiny. But during that time I was developing my connection to the universe, and it has absolutely paid off. When I gave myself time to explore the inner me, I started to dream about the things I wanted to accomplish. I became happy, and that was no magical feat. When you discover who you are and what makes you unique, you begin to show that side of you to the world, finding a peace and happiness from deep within your soul. You've actually been doing this work since you began reading this book, so I'm sure you've already seen some of these deep changes happen in your own life.

Still, some things may seem out of your control. There are many things that make us unhappy: an awful job, a bad relationship, weight issues, health problems. We addressed many of these problems in the previous three chapters; this chapter is designed to help you use psychic energy to take a look deeper within yourself. This will enable you to see your life in a different light and subsequently find the true peace and happiness you deserve.

Through exercises and quick tips you will learn to shed all the things in your life that leave you unhappy or dissatisfied. You will use the universal energy source to release any fear, doubt, or anxiety that separates you from finding peace of mind, and you will use your psychic connection to change your perspective in the areas of your life you dislike, enabling you to live fully in the present moment. Bringing the universal energy to these problems will give you strength to become the happy and successful person you strive to be.

Become Comfortable with Happiness

Finding deep and lasting happiness is an ongoing process of self-realization that begins when you decide to be true to yourself. But you will not find peace and happiness unless you first get rid of everything that is blocking your magic yellow-brick road. That means you must shed any negative thoughts about yourself and your life that may prevent you from feeling comfortable with who you are. You must release any guilt, fear, and self-doubt that stands in your way, and you must forgive yourself for not being perfect.

When you are happy, you love yourself and you are as good to yourself as you are to others. You treat yourself like royalty (which you are!). Some people find it very difficult to be good to themselves, thinking that doing so is selfish or conceited. If this is your problem, the first thing you need to do is become comfortable with the idea that you can love yourself and that you can be happy.

This simple process will wash away any residual feelings of discomfort you feel and balance your energy so you can move forward in your quest for happiness. When you are comfortable with the idea that you can be happy and loved, you will be able to allow yourself to experience that sense of peace and joy. Then you can go on to actively changing any areas of your life that you dislike, enabling yourself to experience true happiness.

Psychic Workout
Becoming Comfortable with Happiness

Do you get queasy at the thought of being happy? Then this exercise is for you. The first thing you need to do is become comfortable with the idea that you can love yourself and that you can be happy. First, suspend any bad feelings you have about yourself for a few moments, and work through the Becoming Comfortable with Your Destiny exercise (chapter 3).

As you visualize a perfect You in the pod in front of you, see yourself as happy, free from constraints, and at peace with the real You. In that moment, let go of other people's expectations of you; let go of any negative feelings that may get in the way of this happiness. While you visualize the perfect You, tell yourself that you love what you see and you love who you are. Tell yourself that you deserve to be happy.

I don't care how difficult this is—just do it. I suggest you practice it two or three times a day until you feel an internal shift in the way you perceive yourself and interact with the world.

Happiness Begins from Within

If you dislike certain things about yourself and your life—your job, your weight, your relationship—you may have a hard time concentrating on anything else. It is hard to love yourself when you are carrying around negative feelings about some aspects of your life that seem to overshadow the good things.

An important part of finding happiness is doing inner psychic homework to uncover the areas of your life in which happiness and self-love already exists, and then applying those deep feelings of love and happiness to the negative areas of your life. Positive feelings transfer to the negative areas of your life, and you begin to feel satisfaction where there was once only pain. The more you connect with that self-love, the more balanced, inspired, and fulfilled you become. Only then will you give yourself the freedom to explore who you are and do the things you want to do.

Discovering and reinforcing the happy and fulfilling areas of your life is a two-part process. First, you work on discovering the areas of your life where love and satisfaction already exist. Do a psychic session and ask yourself questions about what you truly love and appreciate in your life. Some good questions are listed in the following workout. It's possible that you may have very few answers. That's OK—when it comes to this exercise, it's quality, not quantity, that counts. Second, when you know what areas of your life you are proud of and what aspects of yourself you appreciate, it's time to do some positive affirmation work to reinforce those feelings, make them stronger, and apply them to the other areas of your life.

As you do this work, you will begin to see previously negative areas of your life actually falling in line with your positive feelings of love and satisfaction. You will get a promotion, become comfortable with your weight, or see your love relationship shed some of its issues. I know this sounds too good to be true, but trust me on this one. You know the power of a positive thought. Positive thoughts attract positive experiences. Thinking positive thoughts about the areas of your life that were previously negative will attract positive experiences to those areas.

Psychic Workout

Finding Happiness from Within

To discover the areas of your life where love and satisfaction already exist, use one of the information-gathering exercises from chapter 4 and ask yourself two questions:

What do I like or love about myself?
What areas of my life am I proud of and/or satisfied with?

Do the exercise and receive your answers. Now do some positive affirmation work to reinforce those feelings, make them stronger, and apply them to the other areas of your life. Start by closing your eyes, taking a few deep breaths, and getting into a deep meditative state. Feel the love you have for those areas of your life; tell yourself how much you love and enjoy those aspects of yourself and your life. A calm and peaceful feeling should fill your body.

Once you have anchored that deep feeling of love and peace in your body, bring your attention to the first area of your life you dislike and apply those expanded feelings directly to that area. Spend a few minutes infusing the negative area of your life with love and happiness. I love my body; I am proud of my job; I am satisfied with my relationship with my parents.

Happiness Is a Few Simple Steps Away!

When we feel unhappy, it's as though a sense of discontent blankets our entire lives. We end up living in a haze of unaddressed dissatisfaction, when in reality we are not unhappy about everything. Often it is just a small area of life that we are unhappy with, but it is permeating all the other areas, and we think we are totally miserable.

A change in one area of your life can make all the difference. By doing the following five-step exercise, you can pinpoint the areas of your life that you are unhappy about and take the proper steps to change them.

The basis of this exercise is not to accept your unhappiness or discontent. If you are unhappy, there has to be a reason for it, a specific problem that creates gloomy feelings. By using psychic energy to pinpoint these specific reasons and make changes in those areas of your life, you will restore your happiness.

The exercise will also show you steps you can take to make these changes. The steps may be simpler than you can imagine—for example, taking an extra day off from work now and then, buying yourself some new clothes, or taking that trip you thought you couldn't afford might change your entire outlook. You may receive some steps that you feel are too big for you to take, but don't give up. Write a list of all the ways you *can* achieve these specific steps. Writing this list will help ground your goals and will make it easier to achieve happiness. You

Put an Angel on Your Shoulder

When I feel that one of my clients is living with a lot of fears, I recommend that that person surround himself or herself with a shield of protection and put an angel on his or her shoulder. When we live with constant protection like this, we don't limit our thoughts and actions. We take more risks, and we live with a sense of peace and well-being.

Putting a shield of protection around yourself and an angel on your shoulder is a simple ten-second visualization using the universal energy. You get a lot of psychic gusto for that ten-second effort! And you can do this anywhere, anytime, and anyplace you feel the need for some universal support: before you go for a drive, before taking a big test, or every morning before getting out of bed. You can also put protective shields around other people: your friends, family, pets, even your house. This is the last thing I do every night to ensure I get a good night's sleep, and I send protective energy to my friends and family at the same time. I also do this whenever I am in an airplane about to take off. I put a shield around the whole plane and everybody in it.

This exercise really works—sometimes beyond your expectations. One of my clients reported, "Because I feel protected, like someone's watching over me, I don't live my life in fear anymore, and I feel that I can make my decisions in life. I stopped putting up with my old boss's attitude. I said, '———— it!' and started sending out my résumé. I found a new job, with a forty-four-percent pay increase, a better boss, and better learning experience. I actually turned down one good job offer because something said to wait and the right job would come along. The following day I got a phone call, and these people really liked me. I'm not afraid to take chances anymore because I feel I'm being taken care of." Ahhh . . . that's my payoff!

Here's how: Close your eyes, take a deep breath, and call in all the angels and archangels in charge of protection. Ask them to put a protective shield around you. At the same time, visualize a thick, protective shield of white light surrounding you and state the following:

> Only pure energy for my highest and greatest good can enter this protective shield. All energy that is not for my greatest good will bounce off this shield.

Then visualize putting your personal angel on your shoulder (don't forget we all have at least one dedicated just to us!), and say, "Now I am safe and protected."

will also be stretching the limits of your mind by seeing all the ways you can accomplish what you thought you couldn't.

Don't think practically and logically, just write down *every* conceivable way you could achieve your goals. For example, after years of doing private consultations, I really wanted to see some transcending activity in my career. Every time I asked the universe for career direction, I ended up with a ton of stuff to do, but it was always the same stuff. Finally I wrote a list of all the activities I thought of as "transcending" achievements. I didn't think of how improbable they were, I just wrote them. *I could be a consultant on a TV or film project about psychics, I could get a regular contributing spot as a psychic on a TV show, I could give more lectures.* It was only after I wrote out the list that I realized how many things I could do that would step up my career. Now when I talk to the universe, I concentrate on creating the things on this list.

When it comes to creating a happy and fulfilling life, you may find you have all sorts of excuses as to why the things making you unhappy are in your life or why you can't let them go. *I can't leave my job, I have no skills. I can't get a new car, I have no money. I can't go to Europe, it costs too much.* By now you know that you can use psychic energy to get anything and everything you want no matter how illogical or improbable. Excuses will just get in your way.

Psychic Workout
Discovering Your Happiness

Before you begin this exercise, make sure you are already comfortable with the ideas that you can love yourself and that you can be happy. If you are not, do the Becoming Comfortable with Your Happiness workout earlier in this chapter.

When you are ready, start by taking stock of what you are unhappy about and discovering any negative thoughts and beliefs about those areas of your life. Do this by taking out your notebook and writing a list of everything in your life you are dissatisfied with. Go back to chapter 3 and do the What's Not Working in Your Life workout in order to discover what your negative thoughts and beliefs are about each item on your list. Then write a corresponding positive list of beliefs that will help you achieve your happiness. Study that list—make it your own!

Now you are ready to get the universe's help. Pick one of the information-gathering exercises from chapter 4:

Communicating with the Universe
Finding Your Psychic Solution
Magnetizing Information

Get into a meditative state and ask the following questions:

What steps can I take that will enable me to find happiness?
What can I change about my current lifestyle that will enable me to find happiness?

To ground yourself and better achieve these steps, write a list of all the ways you can achieve these specific goals. Then take those steps, concentrating on the actions that will get you where you want to be.

If you sense any resistance to any of the steps in this process, stop what you are doing and work on getting rid of it. Do the Fears and Beliefs workout (chapter 3), asking what fears and beliefs you have about each area of resistance. Create a list of positive Affirmations and Visualizations (chapter 3) to counterbalance the resistance.

AT A GLANCE
Discovering Your Happiness

Step One Take out your notebook and write out a list of everything in your life you are dissatisfied with.

Step Two Do the What's Not Working in Your Life exercise. Discover what your negative thoughts and beliefs are about each item on your list. Write a corresponding positive list of beliefs that will help you achieve your happiness.

Step Three Use one of the information-gathering exercises from chapter 4 to discover the steps you can take that will enable you to find happiness.

Step Four Write a list of all the ways you can achieve these steps.

Step Five Take the actions and add additional appropriate psychic workouts.

Releasing the Negative Feelings That Get in the Way of Happiness

OK, so you've done your homework, but you still experience fear, stress, or anxiety that pops up throughout the day and gets right in the middle of your peace and happiness. Don't stress even more—there is a way to release negativity as it appears before it infects the rest of your day.

Don't Like What You Sense? Clear away Negative Energies!

Have you ever walked into a room or house and felt instantly uncomfortable? Or have you ever suddenly felt the presence of something that you know is not your angel or spirit guide?

There are several explanations for this. That presence or sense of discomfort could be a spirit that is attracted to you or to the place where you are. It could also be negative energy left over from the room's previous occupants' arguments and negative thoughts. You already know that negative and positive thoughts have powers. These thoughts can linger, leaving residue for you to pick up; being around this residue will only serve to confuse you. If you have an uncomfortable feeling about a certain place, you can use the following ritual to change any energy you have an aversion to.

You will need a candle and some dried sage. You can get dried sage or a sage smudge stick (a Native American ritual item) at a herb store or from a herb catalogue. Since sage and incense burn alike, you can substitute one for the other if you wish.

In the space in which you feel uncomfortable, say the invocations for your sacred space and protection (chapter 2). Light your candle and your sage or incense, close your eyes, and take a few deep breaths, getting into a quiet meditative state. Call in your guides and angels to assist you in filling the space with pure universal energy.

Walk around the room with the candle and the sage or incense, sending pure white light to every corner, every window, every door. Ask that any energy there harmonize with the pure universal energy that you are channeling.

If for any reason you are nervous or fearful, release your own negativity before performing this clearing process. When you are finished, take a few deep breaths, thank the universe for its help, and reexamine the energy in the room. I'll bet you feel a big difference.

When you have fear, stress, or worry, the feelings usually arise from not knowing or not being able to control the outcome of a situation you are in. The following repetitive exercise can help you instantly connect with the peaceful and expansive universal energy. Since psychic energy naturally washes away fear as it expands through your body, you will not need to know the outcome of a particular situation to feel peaceful and inspired. In turn, the more calm and centered you are, the more positive the outcome will be.

This exercise is similar to the workouts on transcending karma in chapter 5. After you've finished, you may also want to put a shield of protection around yourself and Put an Angel on Your Shoulder to feel safe and protected as you go about your day.

Psychic Workout
Releasing Fear and Anxiety

Whenever you feel fear, stress, anxiety, or any other negative emotions, take thirty seconds out of your day and find a quiet place. The stairwell, the supply closet, the bathroom—any convenient place will do. Close your eyes and take a few deep breaths.

Visualize a ball of light two or three feet above you and in front of you, so you can see it comfortably in your mind's eye without hurting your neck. It is pure universal intelligence—your angels, spirit guides, your Higher Self, or God. With all your intention, repeat this statement:

Dear universe: I release this [fear, stress, worry, or whatever] to you. Rebalance my energy and restore my well-being. I release this [fear, stress, worry] to you; with that I am at peace.

At the same time, visualize yourself handing the fear, worry, or stress, along with the situation that provoked it, to the ball of light. As you breathe in and out, fill yourself with pure universal energy directly from the ball of light. After a few deep breaths, you will instantly feel calm and balanced. If not, repeat this process one more time.

The Zen of Jumping!

Zen is a Buddhist philosophy of expressing oneness in being, and there are a lot of books out these days that show you how to find the Zen in almost everything we do. My favorite activity is to experience Zen through jumping. I have a lot of energy, and I tend to jump up and down a lot, especially when I get excited. I have discovered there are many ways of jumping up and down: Your arms can go up and down in unison with your jumping; your arms can stay at your sides; you can jump up, down . . . *and* around. I even jump about in little circles. However you do it, jumping is a truly joyous experience. Try it sometime.

When you become focused on an activity like jumping (or juggling or washing dishes), you open your connection to the universe and become one with everything around you. Try doing your affirmations or visualizations or asking for guidance while in this open state. *What is the best outcome to this situation? What can I expect from this opportunity?* There are answers in the Zen of the moment.

Finding the Lightness of the Moment

Lightness, peace, joy—we've all had spontaneous moments talking with friends, watching TV, or walking the dog, where we achieved a natural state of timelessness, where wisdom and grace came effortlessly, where revelations about life and what is truly important became clear to us.

But in the scheme of our lives, these moments seem fleeting. The rest of the time we spend wishing we were someplace else, doing something else. We think about what's going to happen later in the day or over the weekend. The more we distract ourselves and split our attention several ways, the less we deal with the moment that we are presently in. And the more scattered we are, the less ability we have to use psychic energy to change our world.

Many of the exercises we've been doing in this book involve repeating words, phrases, and images to change our experiences. This is because the more you are focused in the present moment, the more you connect with the universe. The more you connect with the universe, the faster you change your experiences. Think back to those expansive moments you've had. One of the reasons those experiences were so expansive and fun is that you were completely focused on what was going on right then and there. You weren't worried about being on time for the big meeting, or whether you were going to close the big deal, or how your test results were going to turn out.

These moments of joy and enlightenment don't have to be saved for an occasional weekend or evening. Here's how to find the present in every moment, enabling you to achieve peace with every situation and to use your psychic ability in every moment.

Whenever you find yourself doing something, anything—at work, at home, at play—and you're only half there, bring your awareness completely to that moment and study it for a second. Observe what is going on and how you fit into the picture, bringing special attention to what you are doing. You may not like what you are doing, and that is why you are thinking about something else, but in that moment just do what you are doing with your complete awareness. Then take note of all the things that you are content with, including something you are happy about, within that situation. Tell yourself that in that moment you are happy. In the split second, your mind is focused in the present; remind yourself that you do not need anything or want anything because you are fully content and taken care of.

When you think about the previous statement, you'll see that you really are peaceful and that your needs are met probably ninety-five percent of the time. Do this exercise two or three times a day. Soon, you will begin to do it automatically. You will find yourself living more in the present, feeling more content, and worrying a lot less. As a byproduct, you will find yourself attracting situations where you can be content and peaceful in the moment. You will find constantly negative situations clearing up and becoming brighter and happier situations. And the more you do this, the more access you will have to psychic energy.

Another way to use this exercise is to observe your thoughts and feelings while you are in situations that usually make you frustrated or anxious. I do it when I am running errands or riding the subway. Instead of grumbling and getting annoyed that I'm stuck in a long line at the bank or on a crowded train, I look around and find the humor in the situation. Sometimes I ask myself what would be the funniest thing I could do at that point in time. Before I know it I'm grinning at something—and I look really ridiculous! By becoming aware of your thoughts and actions in your everyday life, you can choose to think and feel anything you want. Instead of being unhappy in those moments, you can use them as release time, fun time, or healing time.

Give Yourself a Break!

One reason some of us aren't happy is that we are too tough on ourselves. We do things because we feel we should. We work too hard, don't get enough sleep, do everything that is asked of us and more. Instead of finding an easier way, or setting up personal boundaries that others may not appreciate, we make up excuses for our struggles. Or we get so used to struggling that we don't even recognize there is another way.

I used to be so hard on myself. I would get up every morning, pop right up out of bed and go to the gym, then go to work—whether it was writing, doing readings, returning phone calls—I'd have to be busy all day. My life was very regimented. Then a few years ago I got a little lazy. I let myself lie in bed for fifteen minutes before getting up, and if I didn't feel like going to the gym, I'd stay home. I stopped forcing myself to do some of the things that I thought were making me a stronger person, and I was able to find inner peace. Now, instead of doing anything automatically, I live much more in the moment, make spontaneous decisions, and go with the flow. I still get a lot accomplished in a day, I'm just not as stressed as I used to be about being perfect.

The way to discover easier paths is to live consciously, examining all the thoughts and motivations that usually remain unconscious. Seeing the reasons why you do certain things can help you change constructive habits you have fallen into. Once you see what thoughts lead to actions you dislike, you can consciously choose to look at things differently and take another path. So finding a sense of peace may be as simple as changing the way you live your everyday life and adding a few perks. Using your psychic connection to assist you can make this process a lot easier.

As you go about your day, don't unconsciously take the same actions you always do. Reexamine moments of stress, discontent, or unhappiness. If you always get frustrated after meetings with your boss, or you hang up on your mother when she asks who you're dating, stop what you are doing and examine the thoughts that led to those feelings and actions. Close your eyes, breathe deeply, and take a psychic look into the unhappiness. *What choices could I have made to avoid that situation? How could I have treated myself better? What could I have done differently to find a happier outcome? Instead of feeling this way, what other feelings could I choose?*

As you go through your day examining your thoughts, feelings, and actions, don't let excuses get in the way of being good to yourself. If you are tired and want to take a cab home instead of walking—do it. Buy yourself the nicest item instead of the one on sale; take a day off to sleep and let your boss worry about the deadline for a change; visit the old friend you always seem too busy for; go out to dinner instead of making it. Treating yourself better will raise your daily comfort level, increasing your sense of happiness and well-being at the same time.

Spice Up Your Life

You don't always need to make life-altering changes to transform your experience with the world. The things we overlook or take for granted can often be the catalysts for our positive and negative experiences. Instead of leaving these little things unexamined, let them change your life.

One way to do this is by using fun activities or creative work to inspire you, open your channel to psychic energy, add meaning to your life, and be receptors for answers you are looking for. When you feel bored or disconnected, increase the fun activities, wild adventures, or creative outlets in your life, and you will get right back on track.

Singing is a great example of this. I sometimes walk around my apartment singing Broadway show tunes, and I hum all sorts of songs while I work in order to alleviate stress. Singing, humming, and chanting are great ways of connecting to the universe's unlimited supply of energy. Try doing these things during your psychic sessions. Create your sacred space, take a few deep breaths, and chant to yourself with your eyes closed. Use the sounds "oooo" or "om," or use one of your affirmations like a mantra (a phrase repeated over and over again to achieve a meditative state). *I am safe, I am at peace,* or *I am one with the universe* are just a few examples of the many phrases you can chant to open your psychic connection.

Artwork is another channel opener—crayons, pastels, paints; you name it. I like to light a few candles, get into a deep state, contact my angels, and draw their pictures. Or I draw images from my dreams. It doesn't matter how good or bad you are at drawing—you will reap benefits, because creative effort of any kind will allow you a psychic connection. That's what you are striving for, not to become a world-famous artist.

Psychic information and healing can be received while hiking in the woods, playing with an animal, practicing yoga, rock climbing, cliff diving—absolutely anything that you're truly engaged and involved in. By using your psychic connection during activities you enjoy, you give yourself the ability to receive psychic energy in the easiest and most direct manner. Before your chosen activity, sit down, close your eyes, take a few deep breaths, and pose a question to the universe. As you bring your full awareness to the activity and enjoy what you are doing, your connection to the universe will be working as well. When you are finished, take a moment to ground yourself, close your eyes, take a few deep breaths, and write down any revelations in your journal.

Give Your Way to Happiness

Another pursuit that will create happiness and joy in your life—as well as giving you a shot of universal energy—is randomly helping others. By shifting your view from what is going wrong in your life to seeing what you can do to help someone else, you not only stop harping on your unhappiness, you develop a new sense of self-worth.

This is one of the habits I have developed over the last few years. Whenever I am feeling like I am not going to get the things I have worked so hard to achieve, when money is tight, or work seems tough, I stop what I am doing and close my eyes. I take a deep breath and re-mind myself that I am here to help others, and as long as I do that everything will work out fine. Then I ask the universe to put me in contact with someone who needs my help, someone whom it is within my power to help. Lo and behold, within twenty-four hours I usually get a response. I see a mother trying to get a baby carriage down a flight of stairs, or I see a homeless person who could use a cup of coffee and a kind word.

Doing something selflessly is the quickest way to get a boost of psychic energy. When you do something good, you may get a chill up your spine or a tear in your eye. That is a sign from the universe that you have just made a connection. The only catch is that none of this will happen unless you shift your perspective from what is going on within you to what is going on outside of you.

Try playing a game with yourself. Tell yourself you are going to smile at one stranger each day, or commit to saying one kind word to everyone you come in contact with. Every time you connect with others in this way, you connect with psychic energy. At the end of the day, see how happy and energized you feel. Notice the rewards you get by accessing psychic energy this way.

This one behavior is unpredictably contagious! I remember one Christmas, I had some extra cash and I went down the block to the local homeless organization. I said hello to a few of the homeless people gathered outside and offered to buy them a hot dog for the holiday. One wanted catsup, another preferred mustard, a third wanted catsup, mustard, and relish. I took their orders and walked across the street to the hot dog vendor. I ended up making three trips to the vendor before this escapade was over. By the third trip, the vendor figured out what I was up to and said, "Next one's on me." Remember, this is New York City we're talking about!

There you have it: happiness in a nutshell! Now you know that you don't have to trade in your favorite coat for a Hare Krishna robe in order to find inner peace and happiness. By using the universal energy to look within and by reexamining different areas of your life and making subtle changes, you have found that happy isn't something you become: happiness comes in being who and what you already are. By having the courage to love yourself and change the habits and patterns that limit your happiness, you take charge of yourself and your own well-being.

Make a Good-Luck Charm

Carry the universe in your pocket by taking an ordinary object, like a coin, a rock, a feather, or a pendant, and making it into a good-luck charm. A good-luck charm is any object that you think brings you luck—traditionally, these are hard-to-find items, such as four-leaf clovers or horseshoes. To create a good-luck charm, you take a special object and infuse it with the magic of the universal energy. Objects hold energy, especially metal ones, and the universal energy is the purest energy source around. When you carry an object infused with universal energy, you become extra magnetic, attracting all sorts of good things your way.

You can make lucky charms for your friends and family, or focus universal energy into an object in order to attract specific goals, like a safe pregnancy or a good interview. Begin as you would any other psychic session. With your item handy, create your sacred space, take a few deep breaths, and get into a deep, relaxed state. Hold the object of your choice in your hands, and, using your body as a conduit, open up a channel to the universal energy at the top of your head. Pull the energy down through your body, sending it directly into the object. Announce to the universe that you intend this object to hold the highest and purest energy, that you intend the object to be a magnet to attract all good things to you. If you have specific goals in mind, send those vibes into the object along with the pure energy. If you are making a good-luck charm for a friend, make sure you tell the universe who the object is for, so the energy in the object will harmonize with that person.

Spend about three minutes connecting to this object and infusing it with pure psychic energy. When you are through, close your sacred space and end your session. Carry the object with you and see what special things you attract.

chapter nine

psychic shopping and other cool hobbies

I **love shoes.** But I don't love shopping for them as much as I enjoy wearing them. I am not a big browser, so before I go shoe shopping, I usually know exactly what I am looking for; I've seen it in my mind's eye and I am excited to make that vision a reality. I decide ahead of time what to spend on this new pair of shoes, and I generally know where I will find it. I head to the first store that feels right, and when I get there I invariably see the shoes of my dreams—always within the perfect price range.

What I discovered about my shoe-shopping habits is that they are very psychic. I was naturally and unintentionally using my connection to the universal energy to magnetize the perfect pair of shoes and at a predetermined price. When it comes to shoes, I am a psychic shopper!

It's really no surprise that I do my shopping psychically, because when I first began to develop my psychic ability, I found myself naturally putting the principles to work in my everyday life. I learned to use my abilities and spirituality to live better every moment of every day, not just in my psychic sessions. I use them at the gym, at the bank, waiting for a train, and cleaning my bathtub.

This chapter will teach you all the ways you, too, can have a psychic life. You can work on getting a new job while you vacuum. You can attract shorter lines at the post office and the bank. Instead of waiting for the bus, you can get the bus to wait for you. Really! By making your cleaning, commuting, and shopping experiences into psychic experiences, you can enable your life to flow more easily and effortlessly. You'll have more fun doing the things that you *have* to do, and you'll have more time at the end of your day to do what you *want* to do.

You might think that some of this stuff sounds a bit wacky—"Psychic cleaning? C'mon!" I'm not saying you have to do all this stuff every time you leave your house. But once you know how to use psychic energy in your everyday world, it becomes your choice to draw on it whenever you want to feel better or save time, money, and effort.

Live Your Day the Psychic Way

The whole purpose of developing psychic ability isn't to keep it separate from your everyday experience, it is to help you live your life better when you are at work, on a date, or getting your driver's license renewed. The only way to apply your psychic knowledge to everyday situations is to get practical experience making predictions during a normal day.

The key to using your psychic ability is to spot perfect opportunities to do so as you go about your daily activities. Psychic information isn't just going to hit you if you are absorbed in other things, so the more you look for opportunities to use your psychic ability in the course of a normal day, the more chances become available to you.

Ten Unknown Facts about the Universe

One Planet Earth is the cosmic beeper, and all those inconvenient earthquakes are just pages for the Milky Way.

Two There's an intergalactic team of beings here to switch the beeper from vibrate to ring. So if we start hearing some strange bells around the millennium, we'll know it's working.

Three Halley's Comet is the longest Ping-Pong game in all creation.

Four The Big Bang was actually exhaust fumes from the creator's big Harley-Davidson.

Five When man landed on the moon, he was greeted by Caruso in a space suit singing "O Sole Mio."

Six The Northern Lights are really just colossal bug zappers. You think you've got bugs, you should just see what's flying around up *there*.

Seven Einstein came up with his theory of relativity after spending a week with his in-laws.

Eight Men are from Mars, women are from Venus, and Earth is just a big penal colony.

Nine When aliens touched down on our planet in 1954, their first words were, "We mean you no harm, we just came to drop off Pee-wee Herman."

Ten Atlantis is actually a 15,000-year-old strip club in downtown Manhattan.

You'll be surprised how many different ways you can use your intuition once you begin to see the world in this light. Recognizing these occasions allows you to activate your inner senses and make a guess. Pretty soon you will be naturally seeking inner guidance for everything without even realizing it.

As you use your psychic ability in little ways throughout the day, you will become more comfortable making predictions and acting on them. You'll more actively listen to your inner senses and follow them when it matters most. You'll see miraculous things happen: You'll follow a hunch and happen upon old friends, or you'll get a gut feeling to walk in a different direction and steer clear of a potentially dangerous situation.

There are all sorts of ways you can be psychic throughout the day. Your friend gave you a big wrapped box for your birthday—what's inside? You're going out to dinner, and your date is late—what happened? You're going on a short trip—what extra items should you pack? Will you need a bobby pin, a sewing kit, an umbrella? When you spot one of these opportunities, take a deep breath and activate your inner senses. Focus on what you want to know. You will get an instant response.

Here are some other opportunities to use your psychic connection:

- *Phone calls. Don't pick up when the phone rings. As you take a deep breath, ask yourself who is on the other end. In a split second you may come up with a name, a relationship, or what the call is in reference to. The more you do it, the better you become.*
- *M&M's, Skittles, Jujubes, or any candy that has several colors and pieces. Before you pick them out of the bag, one by one, ask yourself or the universe what color you are about to pick out. Reward yourself by eating them!*
- *Elevator banks. This one takes some chutzpah (that's guts in Yiddish). The next time you enter a building with a set of elevators, awaken your inner senses and ask yourself or the universe which elevator will open its doors next. While everyone else is huddled in the center of the elevator bank waiting for the next available one to open its doors, walk over and stand in front of the elevator you picked. Don't hesitate or worry about how silly you look, just do it. The more you take risks with your psychic ability, the easier it becomes to follow your impressions.*

Psychic Shopping

I think shopping has gotten a bad rap. There is nothing unspiritual about it—nothing wrong with acquiring things you love and enjoy.

Who's to say that owning and enjoying clothes, jewelry, or cars makes you selfish and inconsiderate?

Nonsense. Your shopping excursions are just another way to connect with and use psychic energy. When your shopping is done from that place, not only will it become a spiritually expansive activity, but you'll never waste your money and energy again. The universe can help you learn positive shopping techniques that will bring you everything you want, easily and effortlessly. Receiving the benefit of universal energy as you shop makes each shopping excursion an all-around expansive, entertaining, and spiritual experience.

Psychic shopping will do three things for you:

1. *You'll find sale items and spend a lot less money than you planned.*
2. *You'll locate items quickly and easily, not wasting any of your time.*
3. *You'll confirm that all your purchases are beneficial to you.*

I call these purchases "positive purchases." Have you ever bought something, and as you walked out of the store, gotten the sinking feeling that you spent too much money? Do you have a lot of things in your closet that you just never wear and can't figure out why you bought in the first place? Those are negative purchases. When you buy something out of fear or stress; when you buy because everyone else has it; when you spend too much and create debt—you are using negative shopping habits. We've all done this, and it feels lousy. But by making your shopping habits more conscious and bringing your psychic ability into the activity, you can be assured that you will no longer have these deflating experiences.

A positive shopping purchase makes you feel inspired, connected, and special. You buy something because you feel beautiful in it; you spend money on something that is fun and exciting; or you pick up a gift to bring happiness to someone else. Those are positive purchases, or psychic purchases. Anything and everything can be a psychic purchase: any item that expands your happiness, any purchase that will spread love and light, any service that creates healing and oneness has the unconditional stamp of approval from the universe. You can spend a day at the spa; buy a new perfume; have a nice dinner with friends; even rent a limousine and party all night.

There are some definite guidelines for positive and negative spending. When shopping psychically, a purchase cannot be detrimental in any way. It can't endanger you or others, and it cannot occur at the expense of people or the environment. Your shopping must be purely motivated and must be financially comfortable for you. Buying champagne in most cases is a luxury that is fun, expansive, and positive, unless the alcohol will be abused; then it falls into the negative shopping category. Clothes made in sweatshops abroad, no matter how cool or how inexpensive, will never be a positive purchase. You will never be able to use universal energy to buy something to manipulate someone or to cure boredom. Using credit isn't bad, but buying something that puts you into heavy debt is impossible under the laws of psychic shopping.

When you bring your psychic abilities into use while shopping, you first magnetize your shopping list. Visualize the items you want beforehand so that when you get to a store, the universe will offer all the items you want, plus they'll be on sale. You'll end up spending less money and using up less of your time doing it.

Let the universe bring things to you. Very often, the universe knows better than we do. By telling the universe that you are planning a shopping expedition without having a defined want list, you tell the universe, "Bring me what I need; bring me what will make my life easier and more joyful." This works best when you are going to a mall or flea market. When you get to the market, close your eyes, take a deep breath, and open your connection to the universe. Then just stroll through the aisles with your inner connection open and see what happens. You may be attracted to a booth in the back, where you find an antique clock like the one your grandmother used to own or the perfect handmade invitations to the New Year's Eve party you are throwing.

Using the universe when you shop provides an automatic system of checks and balances that ensures that you will always be making positive purchases. Say you're in a store, and you stumble across the perfect knapsack. You're unsure if it is a positive or negative use of your money, so you take a second to ask the universe. Chances are, the psychic You will know that deep down you really hate green and would get sick of that knapsack in two weeks.

Psychic shopping is also a great way to test your intuition. When you need to buy food, shampoo, and paper towels, magnetize your shopping list and then go to a store you are unfamiliar with. Let the universe, your spirit guides, and angels lead you through the store, and see how effortless the shopping becomes. By going to a store you are unfamiliar with, you will see just how much you are directed by your spirit guides and angels.

Psychic Workout
Magnetizing Your Shopping List

The next time you have to go to the store, take a few moments before you leave your house to focus on your shopping list. Close your eyes, take a deep breath, and awaken your magnetic ability as you do with the Magnetizing Your Goals workout (chapter 4). Go through your list, item by item, and visualize yourself finding each one easily and effortlessly. Visualize each item being on sale. When you are through with the first item, go on to the next one. This should take just a few minutes.

Then, when you are shopping, you'll not only find the items on your list on sale, you'll discover that instead of having to search for them, they are right in front of you! Depending on how far you want to take this, you can even light a candle—creating a quickie sacred space—and do a mini psychic session to magnetize your shopping lists before you set out on your trek.

This exercise works with anything and everything. Soap, makeup, cleaning supplies, socks, light bulbs, linens, shoes—you name it.

Psychic Workout
Let the Universe Bring Things to You

Plan a shopping expedition and have the universe tell you what you should buy. A perfect time to use this method is when you are decorating a room in your house or looking for that special gift for a friend. Don't agonize over finding that perfect purchase; the universe knows exactly what is out there and where to find it.

Begin a day or two before taking a trip to the mall or flea market. Close your eyes, take a deep breath, and talk to the universe. Tell your guides and angels that you are going shopping and would like their input on what to buy. Visualize yourself at the market, browsing through all the great stuff. Don't focus on specific items; focus instead on having a fun, smooth experience. Imagine yourself taking home a lot of fabulous items without spending a lot of money. Do this once or twice before your shopping trip.

When you get to the market, take a moment to go within. Close your eyes, take a deep breath, and open your connection to the universe. Let the universe lead you through the aisles of the market. As you shop, notice which items, booths, or stores you are attracted to. Let your intuition guide your wallet, and by the end of your adventure, you'll be surprised by your stockpile. You'll find unique items and great prices, and you'll feel really good about your purchases.

Psychic Workout
To Buy or Not to Buy? That Is the Question!

While shopping, you stumble upon an item that interests you. Is it worth the money? Or will it find its way to the back of your closet and never see daylight again?

The next time this happens, hold the item in your hand and close your eyes. Take a deep breath and awaken your inner senses. Then ask yourself some questions:

Do I really want this?
Do I really need this?
Will I appreciate this?
Is this a positive purchase?

If you get three out of four yes answers, go for it. But note how you feel when you get the answer to the last question, "Is this a positive purchase?" If your body, mind, or soul says no, then listen up.

These questions should only be asked of items that already pass the guidelines for psychic shopping:

- *The purchase cannot be detrimental in any way.*
- *It can't endanger you or others.*
- *It cannot be made at the expense of people or the environment.*
- *Your shopping must be purely motivated and must be financially comfortable for you.*

When I shop psychically, not only do I ask myself these questions, I have what I call an "adoration scale." That is a scale of one to ten of how much I absolutely love and adore the item that I am holding. If you tend to buy too much, an adoration scale will help you narrow down your purchases to the things that are most right for you.

Super Psychic Sex

Somehow I just *knew* that would get your attention!

You can do psychic everything, so why not psychic sex? If you're planning to have sex, you can work with psychic energy before and during the event to make it the most memorable of experiences.

Psychic sex begins the day before an encounter you plan to have. During one of your psychic sessions, affirm and visualize your escapade unfolding with perfection, as you would visualize any of your other goals. In your mind's eye, see yourself and your partner enjoying every last detail. If you have any anxieties about your upcoming encounter, this is a good time to do Releasing Fear and Anxiety (chapter 8) so that you can enjoy your adventure free of fear, doubt, or any other negative feelings.

As your encounter begins to unfold, close your eyes, take a deep breath, and get into a relaxed and meditative state. Getting into a meditative state will bring a whole new level of awareness to the event. You will seem more connected with your partner as well as with the universe. You will have less apprehension and more spontaneity.

I don't want to give you too much to think about while you are busy with more important things. But there are quick ways to use the power of your mind and your connection to universal energy to create magic. In advance, do a mini psychic session and ask the universe how you can best use psychic energy while you are having sex to make it extraordinary. Send your partner some pure universal energy, or use the energy to form a shield of protection around both of you.

Apply some of the principles from chapter 8 to make your sexual encounters expansive and happy ones. You'll find that the Finding the Lightness of the Moment and Spice Up Your Life activities will bring new insight to the activity. You'll need to do some inner research before the encounter, using those sections of the book; reread those sections and ask yourself how they apply to you.

Plan special activities in advance and then experiment in the moment. If your partner likes to play cards, figure out a way to begin your escapade with poker. You may decide to play fantasy dress-up or to focus your awareness on the joy of the moment. By spending a few moments on Spice Up Your Life or Finding the Lightness of the Moment, you'll be creating a fun and fabulous way to express yourself.

There are some great ancient spiritual sex techniques out there. If you like exploring, check out your local bookstore or library for information on the Kama Sutra and tantric sex, for example. Oh, and psychic sex is safe sex. Using universal energy as your shield of protection is nowhere near as effective as using a condom.

Exercise Your Body, Exercise Your Soul

Are you the kind of person who goes to the gym three or four times a week? Do you take hikes or long runs on weekends? Then you can psychically tap into your exercise time and get a two-for-one, using your active physical connection as an active psychic connection as well.

There are two ways to use your psychic abilities while you work up a sweat:

1. Use the time practically to focus on the changes you wish to see in your life. *The gym is a perfect place to focus on any areas of your life that need a psychic overhaul.*

2. Take advantage of your open mind-body connection to add power and strength to your physical workout. *With some minor adjustments, you can do just about all the psychic workouts in this book as you ride the StairMaster, pedal the stationary bicycle, run on the treadmill, or lift free weights.*

To most effectively use your gym time as psychic time, start before you leave for the gym. Take a few moments to think about what you want to accomplish while you are there, just as you would plan your physical workout. Maybe you are currently working on a set of affirmations to create more money or change your career. Perhaps you are doing the pod exercise (Becoming Comfortable with Your Destiny) to change your body. Just as you would bring with you to the gym your lock and a towel, take along whatever you need to do these exercises effectively: your list of goals, affirmations, whatever.

Here are some great workouts that work well at the gym:

- *Affirmations and Visualizations (chapter 3). Repeating positive statements is easy to do while you are using gym equipment. They also make you stronger and give you more stamina. I am strong. I am powerful. You can use any of the ones you are currently working with; it doesn't matter whether they have anything to do with your strength or not. If you are comfortable closing your eyes on the equipment, you can do your visualizations there as well.*

- *Becoming Comfortable with Your Destiny (chapter 3). You've seen me refer to this exercise a million times already, because it works effectively in many different situations. Depending on your goals, you can infuse the perfect You with good health, the perfect relationship, or a great job. You can just as easily pull the pod around you and live the perfect You on the Versa Climber as you can on your couch.*

- *Relaxing with Universal Energy (chapter 2). While you focus on the motion of your body on a machine during your workout, you can send pure universal energy to your bones, muscles, and internal organs. Relaxing them will enable you to get a better workout without any leftover stiffness the next day.*

- *Releasing and transcending exercises. The repetition involved makes these perfect gym material, giving your mind something to focus on while you move your body. Try any of these:*

> The three workouts in understanding and transcending karma (chapter 5)
>
> Understanding Your Health and Releasing the Problems (chapter 7)
>
> Releasing Fear and Anxiety (chapter 8)

Don't forget your own creativity. Make up your own workout/ workout program using the different steps and techniques from all these exercises. Figure out what works best for you, and you will be able to change all the areas of your life with the least amount of time and effort.

You can also record different psychic workout steps on an audio cassette and listen to them as you exercise. You can repeat your affirmations and visualizations this way, too. Try focusing on your goals to the beat of music or the motion of your moving feet. You'll find this double hit of universal energy—working your body and spirit at the same time—will help you to create a great future.

We control when we want to shop, have sex, or go to the gym, so that part of this chapter is a no-brainer. But what about all the yucky stuff that we have to do every day or every week, whether we like it or not? Stuff like doing laundry, vacuuming, running errands, and commuting daily? You guessed it—there is a psychic way to do all that, too. And since we've all got to do these things, I'm going to show you how to get through them with ease and grace—and even get some of your goals, affirmations, and other psychic homework out of the way at the same time. Don't pooh-pooh this before giving it a try—you may find out the daily grind ain't so bad!

Be Psychic While You Wait

Running errands is a part of life. We all have to go to the bank, the post office, or the drugstore, which usually means waiting in line at these places. If you're like me, you hate lines. So why not turn what would otherwise be a waste of time into a productive psychic activity?

There are two ways to use psychic energy while running errands:

1. Attract pleasant encounters. *For example, encountering an old friend or a surprisingly short line while getting your prescription filled will help you go through all your errands with ease and grace.*

2. Make the errands themselves seem more pleasant. *For example, if you start reaffirming your sense of peace while you are waiting to mail a package at the post office, you may get rid of that unpleasant feeling that you could be doing something a lot more fun.*

Let's look first at how you can avoid lines and attract other positive encounters as you go through your daily routine. Running a psychic errand begins before you leave your house. Take a moment to close your eyes, take a deep breath, and visualize yourself waiting at the post office in a very short line. See yourself walking in and being delighted to see that the line is much shorter than usual, so you'll probably be in and out of there in just a few minutes. As you view this scene with your mind's eye, tell yourself that this is exactly what you are going to experience in actuality. Then, on your way to the post office, you may want to affirm to yourself that there will be no line there and that you are going to have a very pleasant experience.

As you run your errands, you will see the difference immediately. But sometimes there is just no avoiding a long line or an uncomfortable situation. In that case, occupy your mind by playing around with psychic energy and doing some of your exercises. You'll find that the situation will seem less stressful, and the waiting will go by more quickly. By using seemingly wasted time to achieve your goals, you free up the time you had previously put aside for your psychic session to do other things you enjoy doing.

Here are some good workouts you can do while you wait:

- *Affirmations and Visualizations (chapter 3). Gear them toward changing specific areas of your life, or gear them toward getting through the wait comfortably.*
- *Psychic Commuting (this chapter). Visualize your commute home; then it won't be as bad as the waiting you're doing on line.*
- *Relaxing with Universal Energy (chapter 2). Send calming psychic energy to each part of your body. You can even send healing energy to a pet or a friend.*
- *Put an Angel on Your Shoulder (chapter 8) and visualize a shield of protection around yourself. This will calm you down and keep you out of trouble!*
- *Have fun by telepathically sending a bit of universal energy to everyone waiting on the line with you as well as the employees working there.*

- *Finding the Lightness of the Moment (chapter 8). Look for the positive aspects of your current experience.*
- *Understanding Your Health and Releasing the Problems (chapter 7). Work on getting rid of any health problems that you may have (or ones that you're acquiring from the waiting-in-line hassle!)*
- *The workouts on transcending karma (chapter 5). If you're going through a rough relationship or situation, a line is the perfect time to talk to the universe and repeat a healing phrase.*
- *Releasing Fear and Anxiety (chapter 8). Release any negative feelings you are working on getting rid of. Or release negative feelings about your errands as they come up.*

My favorite things to do when I get agitated waiting on line are Releasing Fear and Anxiety and Finding the Lightness of the Moment. As I release my agitation and figure out what I am meant to learn, I find that waiting isn't so bad. Besides, by the time I am finished with the psychic exercises, I am at the front of the line anyway.

Cleaning with Psychic Solutions

Doing dishes, vacuuming, dusting. If we want our homes to be relatively pleasant, we have to do these chores whether we like it or not (unless you can afford to hire help!). We tend to avoid housework as much as possible, but it just so happens that cleaning is a perfect opportunity to practice your psychic connection. Using some of the exercises and quickie tips in this book, you can make cleaning a livable, if not enjoyable, experience. And you can get some extra help by using psychic elbow grease.

As you begin your next scheduled cleanup, take a few moments to reexamine your beliefs about cleaning chores. This doesn't have to be done with any fanfare or sacred space. Then reread the section on Finding the Lightness of the Moment (page 217). You may find that the actual act isn't as bad as you've always made it out to be! As you focus on the cleaning at hand and find its good aspects, you may see that this ritual plays a part in your life other than taking up time.

If you still have an aversion to the vacuum, close your eyes, take a deep breath, and do the Releasing Fear and Anxiety workout from chapter 8. Give all your negative thoughts about cleaning to the ball of universal light. Fill yourself with pure, balanced energy. Without any expectations, go on about your mission. When I do my cleaning, I make a deal with the universe. I first affirm to myself that this will be an enjoyable experience and that I will flow through my cleaning chores with ease. After I've brought the universe into the picture, the cleaning isn't half as bad as when I go at it alone.

You can also use the motion of scrubbing and dusting to create change in all areas of your life. I am really serious about this. You may not like cleaning, but it is a big opportunity to complete your daily psychic exercises. Are you working on changing your career or carving your abs? These are great to do while washing dishes:

- *Affirmations and Visualizations*
- *Becoming Comfortable with Your Destiny*
- *Magnetizing Your Goals*

Cleaning time is also a great time to do the repetitive exercises:

- *Transcending Karma*
- *Understanding Your Health and Releasing the Problems*
- *Releasing Fear and Anxiety*

Try combining cleaning with some of the activities in Spice Up Your Life (page 221) such as singing, chanting, dancing, or jumping. I am not embarrassed to admit that I talk to myself when I clean. I describe the perfect Me (from Becoming Comfortable with Your Destiny) and sometimes hum or chant my affirmations. You may think it's

Psychic Commuting

Most of us spend a lot of time commuting—by car, bus, train, or on foot. Some people use this time to sleep; others get work done or catch up on their reading. Here's another alternative: Spend the time working on achieving your psychic goals, or use psychic energy to smooth your commute.

When I told my friend Maureen I was writing this section, she said, "I work with the universe every day on my way to the bus stop so that the bus pulls up exactly as I get there." You can use psychic energy to avoid heavy traffic, get through a traffic light before it turns red—or anything that will make your commute easier.

Start before you leave your house. Give yourself ten seconds; close your eyes, take a deep breath, and open your connection to the universe. Visualize the bus arriving at the bus stop at the same moment you do. Tell yourself that your trip is going to go very smoothly and will be an enjoyable experience. As you go on your way, repeat affirmations such as: *The bus is waiting for me. My drive is flowing very smoothly.* Do this for a few days, and you'll be surprised at how easy your travel becomes.

You can also do your psychic exercises en route. Before you leave your house, take a moment to decide what you would like to accomplish on your trip—whether you are trying to lose weight, magnetize certain goals, or reaffirm a fearless You. Then pack the appropriate lists or exercise steps along with your lunch box.

Quickie versions of the following workouts are just as effective, as long as you keep your focus and intention on what you wish to create or change in your life:

- *Affirmations and Visualizations (chapter 3)*
- *Magnetizing Your Goals (chapter 4)*
- *Becoming Comfortable with Your Destiny (chapter 3)*
- *Rebalance Your Energy, Restore Your Health (chapter 7)*

While you're at it, you can try your hand at receiving psychic directions. Before you leave for your trip, close your eyes and ask the universe the best route for you to take to get to your destination, whether you are driving, walking, or taking public transportation. I have many times avoided traffic jams, accidents, and road construction by doing this for a moment before I begin my trek. If you really want to go all the way, try doing it the next time you are going somewhere and are unsure of the way to go. Close your eyes, awaken your inner senses, and visualize the trip using your psychic ability as your road map.

crazy, but a little craziness goes a long way. I dare you to put some psychic fun onto your sponge!

That just about does it. You now have a fully developed psychic ability and can use it anywhere, at any time, while doing absolutely anything you could possibly think of. You can do psychic ice skating, psychic stir-frying, psychic sleeping, and psychic TV watching. As far as I'm concerned, the wilder the better.

Putting universal energy to work in your everyday life will make your whole life an adventure. You will be happier, more balanced, and more at peace. Best of all, you'll hone your ability to make accurate predictions about anything and everything that is important to you. Find a perfect gift for your mother; pick a restaurant that your date will love; and figure out what your year-end bonus will be the month before you get it. I know you're going to have a great and graceful time living your psychic life!

Put the Universe to Work While You Go Play

Let the power of your psychic sessions continue working after you've moved on to other activities. You can work on getting a new job while reading the newspaper, or focus on getting a new boyfriend while you watch *M.A.S.H.* reruns. All you need is a small piece of paper, a pen, and a new candle.

To begin, write a short, specific description of what you are working toward achieving (one goal per session). Create your sacred space and take a few deep breaths. Awaken your connection to psychic energy and your magnetic qualities (Magnetizing Your Goals, chapter 4). Hold your candle for a few moments and energize it by pulling down pure universal energy through the top of your head, sending it through your body and into the candle. Then light the candle, putting the piece of paper under the candle holder. Spend a few minutes visualizing your goal.

This whole process should take about five minutes. When you are through, leave the special candle burning with your goal paper still lying under it. Close your sacred space and go about your daily activities as you normally would. The energy in the candle will continue to work on achieving your goal. The success of this ritual will become apparent anywhere from a few days to a few weeks later. Be on the lookout for signs from the universe that your goals are coming to you!

afterword:
i predict you'll have
a nice life

K udos to you! Now that you've learned all the ways to use psychic energy to change everything about your life and get any information you wish, you probably think you're finished. But I've got some good news: Now that you've learned all this stuff, I'm going to show you an even easier way to get everything you want. Sorry to do this only now, but trust me on this, you had to do the work earlier in this book in order to be ready for the shortcut I am about to show you.

Once you've reached this point in your psychic development, you should feel comfortable enough accessing and using the energy of the universe that you can condense the steps of the exercises you've learned into one simple little package. That package takes the form of a symbol. For example, to access psychic energy at a moment's notice, I have symbol-ized my spirit guide and the process in the Communicating with the Universe exercise into a multifaceted ball of golden light. Then, I envision placing the ball of light somewhere on or near my body so that I have instant access to it. My spirit guide symbol happens to hover over my left shoulder around my ear. All I have to do when I want an answer to a question is focus on the symbol in that spot and take a deep breath. That automatically opens my connection to the universe, and I can simply ask my question and receive an immediate response.

Using symbol-izing and placement, you will find it easier to get all sorts of information on the fly: when the phone rings and you want to know who is on the other end, or you are late for your date and you can't seem to find your car keys. Accessing this information is as easy as visualizing a carrot dangling in front of your forehead.

These symbols can be useful shortcuts for full-length exercises, as well as anything and everything else that will make your life easier and your connection to psychic energy more efficient. For example, you can symbol-ize your favorite affirmations and visualizations and keep them close to your heart. Symbol-ize the perfect You and wear it around your neck like a charm. Or symbol-ize your guardian angel and sit him or her right on your shoulder for protection. If you can dream it up, you can do it. My symbols have been lifesavers on many occasions. They're invisible, but if you could see them hanging all over me, they'd look like lights on a Christmas tree.

Symbols complement your weekly psychic workouts. I usually use my symbols when I want immediate answers, and I do psychic sessions when I want a deeper experience.

Symbol-izing and Placement

You begin the symbol-izing process by first choosing an exercise you wish to symbolize, then creating a shape that you feel identifies that exercise perfectly. You may find you like squares, triangles, colors, or images, such as that of your angel. Your perfect symbol is whatever feels right to you, no matter how way-out you think it is.

Once you have picked the best symbol for a specific exercise, you are ready to begin applying it to the process. This is easy. Go through your chosen exercise a few times. As you progress through each step, focus on the symbol in your mind's eye, and take one deep breath for each step. You may need to speed up the pace to fit one step into one breath, but that's the point—getting it to happen automatically. Soon you will begin to associate each step of the exercise with the symbol you've chosen and a deep breath. The symbol will then take on the power of the exercise without your having to consciously concentrate on each step of the process. After a few practice runs, you will be ready to use the symbol during your daily routine. Then all you have to do to awaken your connection to the universe is to concentrate on your symbol as you take one deep breath.

Let me take you through the process using an example. In chapter 2 you learned how to get into a basic receptive or meditative state. The steps were:

1. *Create your sacred space.*
2. *Say the invocation of protection.*
3. *Get into a basic receptive, meditative state.*
4. *Recite the invocation to close your sacred space.*
5. *End your session and write in your journal.*

To symbolize this process, first choose a symbol—say a blue triangle. Close your eyes and visualize a blue triangle in your mind's eye. Go through the steps of the process as you normally would. With your mind's eye focused on the symbol, take a deep breath for every step in this process (except the last step, *write in your journal*). After doing this a few times, you will naturally associate the process of getting into a basic meditative state with the symbol of a blue triangle. Once you feel comfortable identifying the symbol with the combined and con-

densed workout steps, all you have to do in order to get into a basic receptive, meditative state is call on that symbol in your mind's eye as
you take one deep breath. Voilà! You have just symbol-ized your first
exercise.

As you know, there are other psychic exercises in this book in
which you open your connection to psychic energy through a cone at
the top of your head, or you use your body as a connective cord to the
energy. When you symbolize these intricate exercise processes, in one
breath you're able to connect to the universe, whereas you used to
take six or seven steps to do so. As you associate each individual step
with your chosen symbol, the exercise becomes instant and unconscious. Just make sure you have the symbol close by in case you need
it pronto.

That leads me to the second part of symbol-izing and placement.
Placement is simply taking a symbol and putting it strategically
around your body so that you have access to it by focusing on that
spot. You can place a symbol on your left shoulder, in front of your
mind's eye, or directly above your head—whatever seems natural to
you. Practice visualizing the symbol a few times to get your mind used
to that spot where you located it. Remind yourself that it's there, and
use it for a few days as you go about your daily routine. Don't worry
about finding the perfect time and place to activate the symbol you've
placed around your body; just use it—you could be at the grocery
store picking out ripe peaches as far as I'm concerned. The more you
use it, the more it becomes part of you. After a little practice, you'll
begin to rely on these symbols in situations that make a difference to
you. *Which of these lines at the drugstore will be the shortest? What's another route to take to the dentist to avoid the construction I see ahead?
Which of these shirts will my friend like best for her birthday?*

You can symbolize exercises you do every day, such as Grounding,
Relaxing with Universal Energy, or Communicating with the Universe. Place them in different places around your body, and when you
are having a bad day at the office and you want to relax, concentrate

on your spot, visualize your symbol, and take a deep breath. Then use the psychic energy to relax. When you are about to go for a big job interview, concentrate on your spot, visualize your symbol, take a deep breath, then ground yourself. When you wish to receive an answer to a question, concentrate on your spot, visualize your symbol, take a deep breath, and telepathically pose your question to the universe. The answer will be right there waiting for you.

Your psychic ability and your connection to the unlimited energy of the universe will always keep you comfortable, safe, and inspired. No matter where you go or what you do, with psychic energy, all things are possible. As you live each day connected to this energy source, you will have the world at your fingertips. Every day will be an adventure, and every day a delight. Go for it!

appendix:
list of psychic workout
exercises

Stacey Wolf, America's youngest nationally recognized psychic, has been featured on *Jenny Jones, Hard Copy, Geraldo,* ABC's *World News Now, Rolonda,
Mike & Maty, America's Talking, Q2 Home Shopping,* and *Fox Midday News.*
She had her first psychic experience at age three; before focusing solely on her
psychic work, she was a successful actress and stand-up comedian, and worked
as a writer and producer at MTV. She is featured in *The 100 Top Psychics in
America* (Pocket) and writes a regular column for *Psychic World* magazine.